DISCOVER THEIR UNDERWATER WORLD!
SHARKS

This edition published by Parragon Books Ltd in 2013

Parragon Books Ltd
Chartist House
15–17 Trim Street
Bath BA1 1HA, UK
www.parragon.com

Edited by Grace Harvey and Philip de Ste. Croix
Designed by Francesca Winterman and Sue Pressley
Cover design by Francesca Winterman
Consultant: Philip de Ste. Croix
Designed, produced and packaged by Stonecastle Graphics Ltd

ISBN 978-1-4723-2448-1

Printed in China

DISCOVER THEIR UNDERWATER WORLD!
SHARKS

Bath · New York · Singapore · Hong Kong · Cologne · Delhi
Melbourne · Amsterdam · Johannesburg · Shenzhen

CONTENTS

INTRODUCTION

Sharks are found in all the oceans of the world.
Some are fierce meat-eaters that rip their prey
to shreds, others feed on tiny plants and animals,
called plankton, that drift along in the ocean currents.

Our planet was formed around 4600 million
years ago. The first living creatures appeared
roughly 1200 million years later. Life in the
oceans evolved slowly until sharks appeared
around 400 million years ago. Since then, sharks
have evolved into over 470 different species.

The longest existing of modern sharks are
the cow sharks (sixgill and sevengill) which date
back 190 million years. These primitive species
can be found in the deep sea. The newest of
modern sharks are the hammerheads, which
are thought to date back 50 million years.
Sharks are among the oldest creatures that have
been living continuously on Earth.

The term 'shark' was first used in 1569 to
advertise a specimen that was brought back to
London and exhibited there. Sailors had caught
it during an expedition to South America,
commanded by the famous Elizabethan
seaman Captain John Hawkins. Why the sailors
called this fish a 'shark' remains a mystery.

Sharks live in various marine habitats around
the world. Most prefer temperate and tropical
waters, but some are found in colder seas
nearer the North and South Poles. They range
from the shallow waters near the coastline right
out to the open ocean, and some even live in
deep waters where light does not reach.

WHAT IS A SHARK?

Sharks are fish that live in the seas and oceans all over the world. There are over 470 different species of shark. They have been living on the Earth for 400 million years. The shape of a shark is so perfectly adapted to living in the water that it hasn't changed much in all that time.

DIFFERENT TYPES OF SHARK

Some sharks are tiny, others are giants. Some are gentle and some are fierce. Some swim very fast to catch their prey in the open sea. Others move slowly and feed on animals that live on the ocean floor.

Fin
Stiff fins are supported by rods of cartilage.

Gills
Gills are used to breathe.

Snout
The snout is often sharply pointed. The mouth is shaped like a crescent.

Did you know?

Inside most fish is an air-filled swimbladder, which keeps the fish afloat. Sharks don't have swimbladders. Instead they have oil-filled livers that help them float. Most, however, have to keep swimming or they sink.

Dogfish have long, slim bodies to slip through the water.

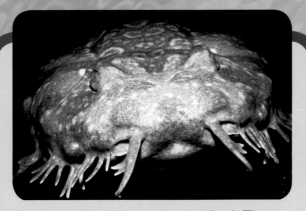

Wobbegongs hide on the seabed. They are well camouflaged.

Tail
A strong pointed tail fin pushes the shark through the water.

Angel sharks have flat bodies. They also hide on the seabed.

Basking sharks live in open water. They are often seen swimming quite close to the coastline.

AMAZING SHARKS

Can you imagine a fish that has a head shaped like a hammer? Or one that can gobble up a sea lion whole? Sharks are some of the world's most amazing creatures.

Great white shark

The great white shark eats other sharks for dinner – along with whole penguins, seals and sea lions.

Whale shark

The gentle whale shark is the world's biggest fish. It weighs as much as two elephants and can grow longer than a bus.

Mako shark

The bullet-shaped mako shark can swim at over 70 kilometres per hour. It is one of the fastest fish in the ocean.

Hammerhead shark

The hammerhead shark has eyes on each side of its head. It swings its head from side to side to get an all-round view.

Did you know?

Sharks don't have bones. Their skeletons are made from light, stretchy cartilage. This is the same kind of material that humans have in their ears and noses.

Hammerhead sharks have smaller pectoral fins than other species of shark.

TEETH

Teeth are a shark's most important weapon. They are designed to help it catch and eat prey.

Sharks have multiple rows of teeth. Every time a shark loses a tooth, the tooth in the row behind it moves forwards to take the lost tooth's place.

The shape of a shark's tooth depends on its diet. Sharks that eat fish have long, narrow teeth for gripping slippery fish. Sharks that eat mammals, such as seals, have sharp, jagged teeth for ripping flesh. Sharks that eat shellfish have thick, plate-like teeth to crush the shells of their prey.

Sharks' teeth are not rooted in the jaw like ours, but are attached to the skin covering the jaw.

Unlike most animals' jaws, both the shark's upper and lower jaws move. It bites with its lower jaw first and then its upper.

The great white shark has sharp, pointy teeth, perfect for ripping flesh.

The prehistoric shark Megalodon may have been up to 20 metres long. Here is one of its huge teeth next to the tooth of a modern shark.

The powerful tail of a great white shark helps propel it through the water, to attack prey.

The small cookie-cutter shark swims up to a larger fish, takes a bite out of its side (the shape of a cookie), and swims away again very quickly!

HOW SHARKS SWIM

Dorsal fin
The stiff fin on a shark's back helps with balance.

Most sharks are graceful and powerful swimmers. Their smooth bodies are perfect for moving underwater. Sharks swim in S-shaped movements, powered by their tails.

Tail
The shark's tail is a bit like its motor. It sweeps it from side to side in long strokes to power its body forwards. The streamlined shape of the shark's body helps it to glide through the water. Sharks with large tails can accelerate very quickly.

Pectoral fins
Fins on each side of a shark's body help it steer.

Did you know?

Sharks cannot swim backwards. This is because a shark's stiff pectoral fins cannot bend upwards like most other fish, so they are unable to back up.

Fins
The dorsal fin on the shark's back acts like the keel of a boat. It stops the shark from rolling over in the water. The pectoral fins on the sides help to move the shark up and down in the water, like the wings of an aircraft.

Types of tails

The tail fins of sharks vary a lot in shape and size. The top half of the fin is usually larger than the bottom half because the shark's backbone extends into the upper half of the fin.

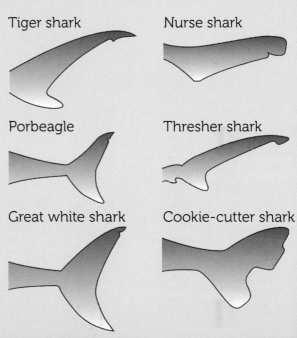

Tiger shark

Nurse shark

Porbeagle

Thresher shark

Great white shark

Cookie-cutter shark

Tail

A shark's long tail beats from side to side, pushing the shark forwards through the water.

Slow motion

Whale sharks are slow swimmers, cruising along at about 5 kilometres per hour. They swim by moving their entire bodies from side to side, not just their tails.

Thresher shark

The thresher shark has the longest tail of any shark – its upper part is almost as long as the rest of the shark's body. When hunting fish, thresher sharks are known to 'slap' the water with their tails to stun their prey before eating it.

SENSES AND HUNTING

Sharks are always seeking out their next meal. They can see, hear, touch and smell, just like people. But their senses are much more powerful than ours, and are perfectly adapted to working in water.

Touch

Finding food

A shark uses all its senses to find prey, but smell gives some of the most important clues. A shark can smell a tiny amount of blood in the water from hundreds of metres away.

Touch

A lateral line along their sides helps sharks pick up movements in the water around them.

Hearing

A shark's ears can hear sounds travelling through the water. The ears lie beneath small holes in the shark's head.

Extra sense

Sharks have special jelly-filled receptors in their heads. These extra sense organs let sharks pick up the faint electric signals given off by fish. This sense is particularly powerful in hammerhead sharks.

Sight

Smell

Hearing

Sight

A shark's eyes can see well in dim underwater light.

Smell

A shark does not breathe through its nose. It is just used for detecting smell.

MOTHERS AND PUPS

All baby sharks are born from eggs and are known as pups. The eggs of most sharks grow inside their mother. A few kinds of shark lay their eggs on the seabed, safe inside tough egg cases.

All sharks are born from eggs that are fertilized by sperm from the male shark. But the eggs can grow in different ways. In some sharks they remain inside the mother's body and hatch inside her. The young shark pups are then born as live fish ready to swim away.

Other sharks lay their eggs inside tough, leathery egg cases in the water. The pup grows inside the egg case feeding on the yolk inside it. When it is ready to be born, the young shark wriggles its way out of the case, which splits open.

Little hammerheads
Baby hammerhead sharks are born with their heads bent backwards, so they don't get stuck inside their mother.

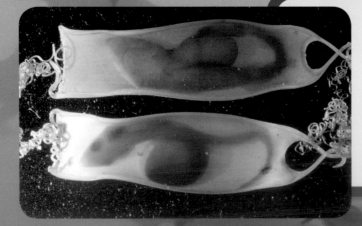

Egg cases
Dogfish eggs are protected by an egg case called a mermaid's purse. The babies grow inside, feeding on the egg yolk.

A blue shark mother can give birth to 50 or more babies at a time. The record for this shark is 135 pups. They take from 9 to 12 months to grow big enough to be born.

Groups of sharks

Sharks do not remain in a family group. When sharks are seen together in a large group, it is usually because a lot of food is available to be eaten.

Lemon sharks

Lemon shark eggs grow inside their mother. She gives birth to tiny pups, which soon swim off to find food. They remain in fairly shallow water while they grow to their adult size of around 2 metres long. This can take between 12 and 15 years.

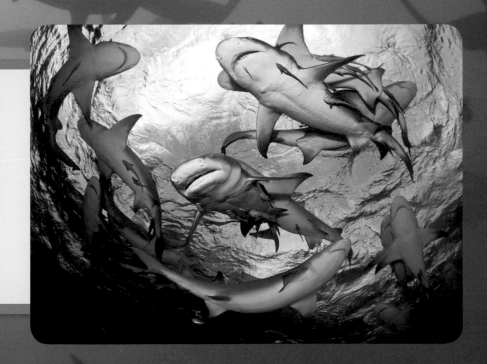

THE SHARK'S WORLD

Our Earth is often called the blue planet because more than two-thirds of its surface is covered by water. Most of this water is found in the oceans. This is where the sharks have their home. They live in shallow waters around the world's coasts, and in deeper water all the way down to the ocean floor.

THE OCEANS

There are five oceans. The largest is the Pacific Ocean, which stretches between North and South America, Australia and the eastern coast of Asia. The smallest is the Arctic Ocean, which surrounds the North Pole. All five of the world's oceans are connected. Smaller areas of water, called seas, are joined to some of the oceans. These include the Caribbean, Mediterranean and North Seas.

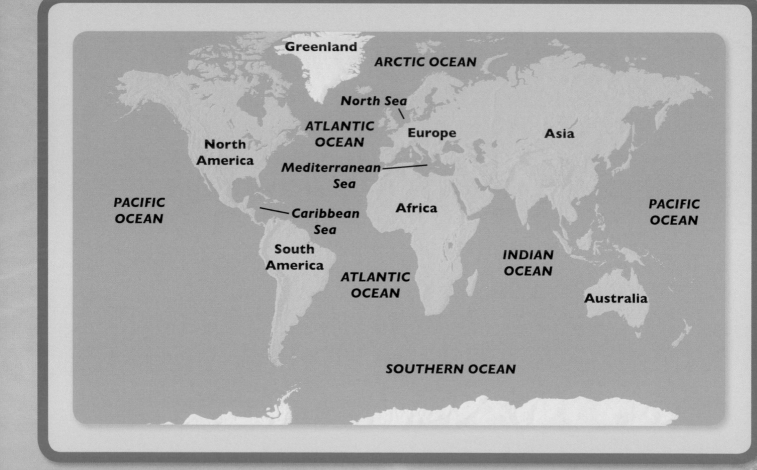

Ocean islands

Oceans are mostly wide, open areas of water. Islands are scattered across the oceans. These pieces of land rise up from under the water. Islands may cover large areas of land or just a few square kilometres.

A small island in the Indian Ocean.

Coral reefs

Coral reefs are found off coasts and around islands in tropical parts of the world. Reefs are home to many kinds of fish, including reef sharks, and other colourful marine animals.

Coral reefs are built from the skeletons of tiny sea animals.

Did you know?

Sharks play an important role in keeping our oceans healthy. Most sharks are at the top of the food chain, and they eat old or sick marine animals. The animals that survive are the fittest ones.

SHARKS IN ANCIENT TIMES

Humans have been exploring the world by sea for thousands of years. Sharks have always been a danger to people whose work takes them out onto or into the ocean. Nearly 2000 years ago, the ancient Roman author Pliny wrote about sharks attacking men who were diving for sponges.

Hawaiian myth

Sharks have been both feared and worshipped by human beings since ancient times. In Hawaiian myth a shark god created the universe and everything in it.

Ancient bond

Humans have collected sharks' teeth for thousands of years. People used to believe they would give some of the unique predatory abilities of sharks.

Did you know?

When the dinosaurs' cousins, the plesiosaurs, went extinct, prehistoric sharks became the main predators in the oceans. They have evolved into the sharks we know today.

WAVES

Waves are created by wind blowing over the surface of the water. The stronger the wind, the bigger the waves. Waves travel across the ocean, just like ripples cross a pond. When waves reach shallow water near a coast, they slow down and become taller. Finally, the top, or crest, of the wave topples over and crashes down onto the shore.

Tsunamis

Tsunamis are waves created by earthquakes under the water. By the time the waves reach the coast, they may be many metres tall. Powerful tsunamis can cause a lot of damage.

In 2004, ships destroyed by a tsunami in Thailand landed over 1 kilometre from the coast.

Did you know?

Sharks have been seen riding inside big waves coming to shore like surfers do.

Surfing

Riding a surfboard on the crest of a wave is an exciting sport. Skilled surfers can twist and turn, jump in the air and ride their boards right under the wave as it rises up and curls over. Quite a lot of shark attacks happen when a shark takes a bite out of a surfer or his board.

TIDES

Twice a day, the sea rises up a shore and then falls back again. High tide is when the sea reaches its highest point up a shore and low tide is when it is at its lowest point on the shore.

Low tide

At low tide, the sea exposes the whole of the shore. In some places, the difference between high and low tides is great, but in others it is very small.

The Sun and the Moon

The tides are caused by the pull of the Sun and the Moon. This pull is called gravity, and it pulls the Earth's oceans towards the Sun and Moon. This creates a bulge of water that produces the high tides. At the same time, there is less water in other parts of the ocean and this is what causes the low tides.

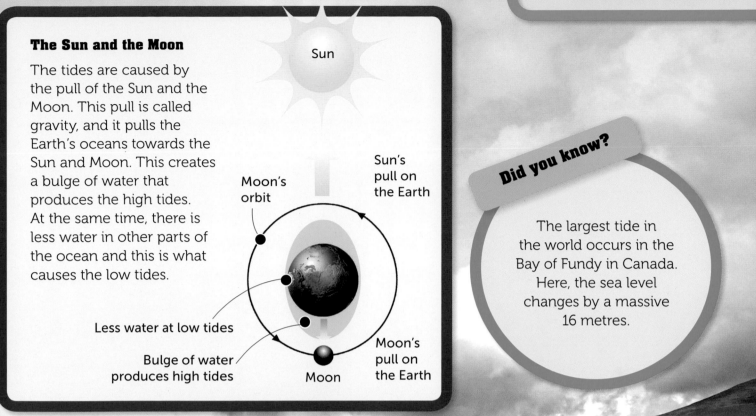

Sun

Moon's orbit

Sun's pull on the Earth

Less water at low tides

Bulge of water produces high tides

Moon

Moon's pull on the Earth

Did you know?

The largest tide in the world occurs in the Bay of Fundy in Canada. Here, the sea level changes by a massive 16 metres.

Sharks at low tide

Sharks can get caught out by tides. They sometimes get stuck in lagoons and small bays during low tides. They are unable to get back to the open sea. People swimming in lagoons at low tide need to keep an eye out for sharks.

BULL SHARK

The bull shark is a fierce predator that will eat almost anything that it comes across. It is solitary, usually choosing to hunt by itself.

The bull shark is large and looks broad because it has a wide body. It is coloured grey on top and off-white below.

It is one of the few sharks that can live in fresh water. Bull sharks are often seen in rivers and lakes. One was even spotted 4000 kilometres upstream in the Amazon River in Iquitos, Peru.

Bull sharks eat all sorts of animals in the water and this includes other sharks, especially the sandbar shark. They sometimes use a 'bump and bite' technique, headbutting their victim first before biting it.

Bull sharks are one of the most dangerous sharks to humans because they are aggressive and often come into shallow coastal waters where people swim and surf. Many of the recorded attacks on people have been made by bull sharks.

Snout
This is wider than it is long, which is unusual for a shark.

Body
The bull shark has a much wider body in relation to its length than most other sharks.

Profile

Length:	Average 2.1 m (males), 3.5 m (females)
Weight:	Average 90 kg (males), 130 kg (females)
Order:	Ground sharks
Family:	Requiem sharks
Diet:	Fish (including other sharks), dolphins, turtles, birds, invertebrates

Location

Bull sharks are found worldwide in the coastal waters of tropical and subtropical (more than 18 °C) seas, and sometimes in rivers. They swim from the surface to about 30 metres deep.

Coastal | Oceanic

Sunlit Zone: 0–200 m

Twilight Zone: 200–1000 m

Midnight Zone: 1000–4000 m

Lower Midnight Zone: 4000–6000 m

OCEAN CURRENTS

Oceans are never still. Flows of water in the oceans, called currents, travel around the world. Currents of warm water flow from the equator towards the poles. Cold currents start in the Arctic and Antarctic and flow towards the equator.

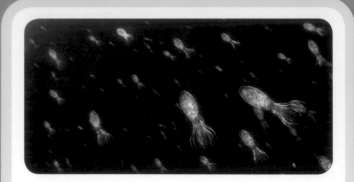

Plankton

Sometimes, an ocean current brings up lots of food from the sea bed. Tiny plants and animals, called plankton, feed well and increase in number, forming a plankton bloom. A plankton bloom can change the colour of the water and measure several hundred kilometres across.

Long-distance swimmers

Blue sharks are long-distance travellers along the ocean currents. Moving eastwards across the North Atlantic female blue sharks have been monitored apparently riding the strong currents to conserve energy.

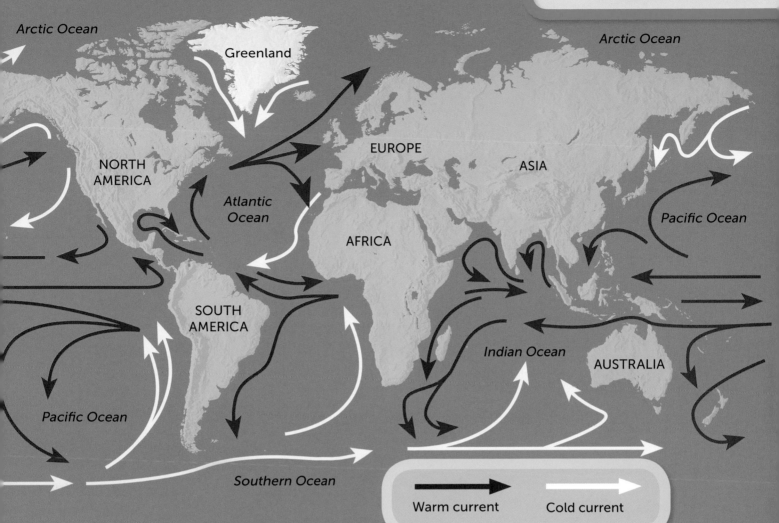

Arctic Ocean

Greenland

Arctic Ocean

NORTH
AMERICA

EUROPE

ASIA

Atlantic
Ocean

Pacific Ocean

AFRICA

SOUTH
AMERICA

Indian Ocean

AUSTRALIA

Pacific Ocean

Southern Ocean

Warm current   Cold current

Did you know?

The Gulf Stream is an ocean current that flows across the Atlantic Ocean from the Caribbean Sea to western Europe. It measures about 80–150 kilometres wide.

Lots of fish

Some ocean currents are high in nutrients, and encourage plankton to grow. This attracts fish that feed on the plankton. The large numbers of fish attract predators such as seabirds.

OCEAN WEATHER

Oceans play an important role in the world's weather. Tropical storms, hurricanes and water spouts all form over water.

Storm clouds gather over the Caribbean Sea.

Tropical storms

Rain falls most days in the regions nearest the equator, called the tropics. Storm clouds form off the coast during the day and bring a heavy downpour of rain at night.

Did you know?

It seems that sharks are able to sense the approach of storms. Different species of shark have been spotted swimming towards deeper water in the Caribbean Sea as a hurricane was moving their way.

The eye of the hurricane

Hurricanes

Hurricanes are huge, spinning storms that form over warm water. Strong hurricane winds with speeds of up to 320 kilometres per hour can cause a lot of damage if they move on to land.

Water spout

A water spout is a spinning column of air and water that moves over water. It looks just like a miniature tornado. Although a water spout is not as dangerous as a tornado, it can damage small boats.

A water spout viewed from an aircraft.

Monsoon

Each year, winds from the Indian Ocean bring heavy rain to South-East Asia. These winds are called monsoons and they last several months. The monsoon season ends when the winds change direction and blow away from land.

Monsoon rains falling in India.

Bull shark

Bull sharks swim close to shore, and in freshwater rivers and lakes. For this reason, they are likely to encounter people swimming and fishing. Its mouth is packed with hundreds of sharp triangular teeth.

SALT WATER

Seawater tastes very salty. This is because the water contains a lot of dissolved salt. Humans cannot drink seawater because it makes them ill. But animals that live in the sea have ways of coping with the high levels of salt.

Coping with salty water

Sharks can get rid of any excess salt that they injest. A gland at the end of the intestine absorbs salt from the blood and it is then excreted.

Adding more salt

Some of the salt in seawater is made when rocks break down, and from hot-water vents on the ocean floor. Volcanic eruptions underwater also add salt to the oceans.

Clouds of steam pour from an undersea volcanic eruption.

Sharks have evolved to live in sea water.

Turtle tears

Turtles have a salt gland behind their eyes. By getting rid of salt through their eyes, nostrils or tongue, turtles can live in salt water without becoming ill.

Salt pans

When salt water gathers in shallow ponds the water dries up, leaving behind large areas of salt called salt pans. The salt can be collected and used for cooking.

Did you know?

The water in the Dead Sea in the Middle East is ten times saltier than in the oceans. This is because the sea has no outlets (such as rivers or streams). This means the salt cannot be carried away.

Dry salt is left when the water evaporates away.

LIVING IN WATER

Animals that live in water are called aquatic animals. Their bodies are adapted to life in water. Fish have gills to breathe underwater, while seals have flippers to help them swim.

Sharks

Sharks are fish, and they breathe using gills. Water enters through their mouths and passes through the gills, where the oxygen is removed. The oxygen goes into the shark's blood stream and is pumped around the body by the heart. The water is pumped out of the shark's body through the gill slits back into the sea.

Gills are used to breathe.

Did you know?

Some sharks are not able to pass water through their gills unless they keep swimming forwards. This means they cannot rest, but must spend their whole lives swimming in order to breathe.

Crabs

A crab has a heavy outer skeleton covering its body. The crab's body is flat so that it can easily squeeze under and between rocks. Crabs have gills inside their shells and can breathe underwater like fish.

Jellyfish

Jellyfish have a soft body made mostly of water. They must stay in water to keep their shape. If you take a jellyfish out of the water, it will collapse into a blob of jelly.

Seals

Seals are marine mammals with flippers instead of arms and legs. Although seals live in water, they breathe air and have to return to land to give birth.

Seals have to come up to the surface to breathe air.

FOOD CHAINS

A food chain shows how nutrients pass from plants to animals as one eats the other. In the ocean, plant plankton is eaten by animal plankton, or zooplankton. The zooplankton is eaten by larger animals. These animals are then eaten by even bigger animals. Many sharks have a diet of seals, turtles, fish and even large seabirds. Some sharks, however, such as the whale shark and basking shark, eat plankton and small fish.

Plant plankton

Plant plankton are at the bottom of the ocean food chains. They are called producers because they make their own food using sunlight.

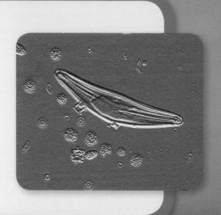

Top meat-eaters

Top carnivores, or meat-eaters, such as pelicans, sharks and dolphins, eat fish. A top carnivore is an animal that no other animal eats – they are at the top of the ocean food chain.

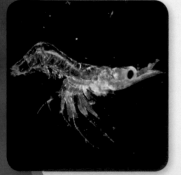

Plant-eaters

Zooplankton, or plant-eaters, such as this crab larva, eat the producers, or plant plankton. The plant-eaters are known as primary consumers.

Meat-eaters

Larger animals called the secondary consumers eat the primary consumers. Secondary consumers are hunters. There are many different hunters in the ocean, including fish and squid.

This great white shark has leapt out of the water to catch a seal.

The darker shade of this shark's back blends with the sea, so that it can attack prey from below.

Did you know?

The great white shark attacks its prey from below. It swims until it is only a few metres away, then attacks by turning its head upwards and surging up through the water.

BENEATH THE SURFACE

Imagine if you could walk into the sea from a beach. First you would walk through the shallow water of the continental shelf that extends out from the coast. Then the sea bed slopes down for thousands of metres to the deep ocean floor.

Ocean levels

In some places the continental shelf is narrow, but in others it stretches for hundreds of kilometres. The continental slope links the continental shelf with the ocean floor, which may be thousands of metres down.

Sea level

Continental shelf

Sea lions

Sea lions swim in the shallow water close to the shore above the continental shelf. They like to pull themselves out of the water and lie on sandy beaches.

Starfish

Starfish are found on the continental shelf. They crawl over the sand hunting for mussels and other shellfish to eat.

Did you know?

The deepest-known part of the ocean is the Mariana Trench in the Pacific Ocean. It lies 11 kilometres below sea level.

Wide-set eyes help the hammerhead shark see above and below at all times.

Hammerhead shark
Sharks, such as this hammerhead shark, are found in both shallow and deep water. Some sharks can dive down several thousand metres to the bottom of the oceans.

Different creatures are found at each depth of the ocean.

Spider crab
Spider crabs are creatures of the sea bed. They have been found on the ocean floor more than 3000 metres below the water's surface.

Continental slope

Ocean floor

TIGER SHARK

Tiger sharks get their name from the stripes and spots that cover the bodies of their young. It also reflects their reputation as large and powerful hunters of the seas.

Tiger sharks are grey-brown on top with a light yellow to white underside. These sharks are some of the largest predatory fish in the seas — the biggest can grow up to 5.5 metres in length and weigh more than 800 kilograms.

Tiger sharks have been called 'the dustbin' of the oceans as they will eat almost anything. Strange items like rubber tyres, bottles, rolls of chicken wire and even a crocodile's head have been found in the stomachs of dead tiger sharks.

These sharks are solitary hunters, mostly searching for food at night. They generally swim quite slowly when hunting prey, but can put in a rapid burst of speed for a vital few seconds when they want to launch an attack.

Teeth
Teeth have sharp jagged edges that can tear and rip virtually anything — even the shells of turtles.

Profile

Length:	Average 3.2 m (males), 2.9 m (females)
Weight:	385 to 635 kg (males and females)
Order:	Ground sharks
Family:	Requiem sharks
Diet:	Fish (including other sharks), turtles, crabs, clams, dolphins, seals, seabirds

Tail fin
The upper part of the tail fin is very long —perfect for swimming quickly as the shark moves in for the kill.

Location
The tiger shark is found worldwide in tropical (more than 18 °C) and some temperate (10 to 18 °C) waters, from the shoreline to the open sea. They swim from the surface to about 340 metres deep.

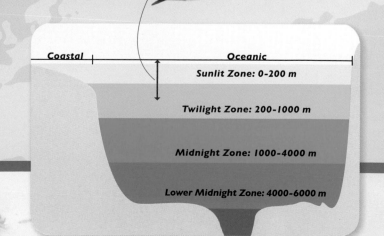

Coastal | Oceanic

Sunlit Zone: 0–200 m

Twilight Zone: 200–1000 m

Midnight Zone: 1000–4000 m

Lower Midnight Zone: 4000–6000 m

DIVING WITH SHARKS

People cannot live in water, but they can dive underwater, using special equipment to help them breathe.

Shark cages allow divers to get very close to large sharks without putting themselves in danger. The sharks are attracted towards the cage by the presence of dead bait fish. However, sharks do sometimes show signs of aggression and may attack the cage.

Shark cage

Discovering wrecks
Shipwrecks in shallow water are popular dive sites. By exploring a wreck, divers can learn a lot about the history of the ship.

Exploring reefs

Many divers like to explore coral reefs. These are good places to find brightly coloured fish and other marine creatures, such as dolphins and sea turtles.

Did you know?

Sharks are not normally aggressive around divers. If a shark gets too close to a diver, it is sometimes possible to scare it away just by pushing on its nose, which is very sensitive.

Breathing underwater

Scuba divers carry a tank of air to help them breathe underwater. The tank is connected to a regulator, which the diver places in his or her mouth. When the diver breathes in, air flows through the regulator into the mouth.

Regulator

Tiger shark
This is one of the largest sharks living today. It has spots and stripes on its body, particularly when young. These fade as it gets older. It hunts mainly at night and will eat almost any large sea creature that crosses its path.

EXPLORING THE DEEP OCEAN

The deep ocean is very cold and the huge pressure would crush a human instantly, but some sharks can be found at depths of more than 3500 metres. Scientists use hi-tech equipment to explore this part of the ocean.

Underwater features

Using technology, such as submersibles, scientists have made maps of some of the ocean floor. They have found mountain ranges, such as the Mid Atlantic Ridge, and deep valleys, such as the Mariana Trench in the Pacific Ocean.

This map shows some of the mountain ranges that lie underwater on the ocean bed.

NORTH AMERICA

SOUTH AMERICA

Submersibles

Submersibles are specially designed mini submarines that can dive to depths of 11 kilometres. Inside there is room for only two or three people.

This submersible has a strong frame made from titanium metal up to 5 centimetres thick.

EUROPE

Atlantic
Ocean

The Mid Atlantic Ridge
runs down the middle
of the Atlantic Ocean.

AFRICA

ROVs

Remotely operated vehicles (ROVs) are controlled from the surface of the water. These vehicles have mechanical arms to pick up objects, and cameras to film any strange creatures.

Deep-sea creatures

Scientists have discovered amazing creatures living deep underwater. They include seastars, blind shrimp-like creatures called amphipods and comb jellies, which can produce their own light.

Did you know?

The record for the deepest living shark is held by the Portuguese shark which has been found at a depth of 3675 metres. It feeds mainly on fish, octopuses and squid that live near the ocean floor.

COASTAL SHARKS

The shallow waters around land are full of life. Here, tiny plants called phytoplankton and animals called zooplankton float in the water. Amazingly, the two biggest sharks of all feed on these tiny organisms.

TINY PLANTS

The moving ocean stirs up mud on the seabed. This releases nutrients into the water. These nutrients provide food for tiny plants called phytoplankton that float in the water.

Phytoplankton

Phytoplankton sit at the bottom of the food chain and sharks at the top of it. But the two biggest sharks, the whale shark and the basking shark, feed on these tiny organisms. They filter them out of the water with bristly rods called gill rakers.

Did you know?

Just like plants on land, phytoplankton can make their own food using sunlight, carbon dioxide (a gas) and nutrients from the water.

Whale shark

Slow-moving whale sharks scoop up plankton near the surface of the water. These sharks have no teeth. They are called filter feeders.

Diatoms

Diatoms are a type of phytoplankton that have hard, shell-like skeletons. The skeleton is in two parts, called valves, that fit together tightly. There are many types of diatom, each with its own design of skeleton.

Plankton bloom

Phytoplankton are able to grow and reproduce very quickly. They can treble in numbers in just one day. Sometimes, there are extra nutrients in the water and the phytoplankton increase in number. There are so many plankton that the water changes colour. This is called a plankton bloom, and it can grow so large it can even be seen from space.

This large plankton bloom is off the coast of Argentina.

Dinoflagellates

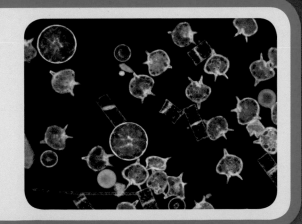

Dinoflagellates make up much of the phytoplankton. At night, these tiny organisms give out a strange light. This is called bioluminescence.

TINY ANIMALS

Phytoplankton are eaten by the creatures that make up the animal plankton, or zooplankton. These animals drift in the water, carried around by tides and currents.

Shoals

Fish sometimes hunt for food like plankton in large groups called shoals. These shoals attract larger predators, like sharks, farther up the food chain.

A blacktip reef shark approaches a large shoal of reef fish on which it can feed.

Microscopic creatures

Most animal plankton is made up of tiny shrimp-like creatures called copepods and amphipods. The larvae (young form) of marine animals such as starfish, jellyfish and barnacles are also called animal plankton.

Jellyfish

Jellyfish are among the largest animal plankton. They have a bell-shaped body and long tentacles, which hang below. Many just drift in the water, while others swim by flapping the skirt of their body.

Salps

Salps are tube-like organisms about the size of a large peanut. They suck in water and food at their front end. The food goes to the stomach while the water is pumped out at the back. This is what makes the salp move forwards.

Baby fish

Many fish lay their eggs in coastal waters. When they hatch, the baby fish feed on phytoplankton that are floating in the water around them. The small fish grow quickly until they are large enough to swim away from the coast and out to sea.

Salps may link together to form chains that are up to 5 metres long.

PLANKTON FEEDERS

Animal and plant plankton are the favourite food of many animals including ocean giants such as the whale shark and basking shark. Most plankton feeders filter, or sieve, tiny organisms from the water.

Basking shark

The basking shark swims along with its mouth wide open. When its mouth is full of water, the fish closes it and squeezes the water out through its gill slits. Any food is trapped inside by rakers (bristle-like filters) in the gills.

Manta ray

Most rays live on the seabed, hunting fish and small animals. The huge manta ray is different. It is an active fish that swims great distances, filtering plankton through its gills.

Did you know?

Scientists believe that some whale sharks may live for up to 180 years. Male whale sharks are not ready to start breeding until they are around 30 years old.

Humpback whales have frilly plates called baleen in their mouths that sieve the water.

Whale shark

The whale shark is the largest fish in the world. It usually grows up to 12 metres long and can weigh more than 20 tonnes. It is a filter feeder and, despite its size, it is not a dangerous shark to humans.

A whale shark's spots are unique, and can be used to recognize each shark.

BASKING SHARK

This incredible-looking shark is the second largest fish (after the whale shark) in the oceans. It may look frightening, but this is a gentle giant. It feeds on tiny plankton as it cruises slowly near the surface.

The body of the basking shark is greyish brown to dark grey, sometimes with lighter patches on the flanks. Its head is quite pointed, but as soon as the shark starts to feed, its appearance changes dramatically. Its huge jaws gape open to allow water to pour over the gill rakers inside its throat. These trap the tiny particles of plankton on which it feeds. This is called filter feeding. More than 1.3 million litres of water – enough to fill two Olympic-sized swimming pools – pass over its bristly gill rakers an hour.

Basking sharks feed near the surface where the tiny plankton organisms are attracted to the sunlight. They are seen fairly often off the coastline by fishermen. Basking sharks migrate thousands of kilometres during the winter months, seeking clouds of plankton (called blooms) in warmer waters.

Mouth
A huge mouth like an enormous butterfly net sweeps up tiny food organisms in the water.

Large gill slits
Bristles behind the gill slits, called gill rakers, trap food particles in the water.

Profile

Length:	4 to 5 m (males), 7.5 to 9 m (females)
Weight:	Up to 3900 kg (males and females)
Order:	Mackerel sharks
Family:	Basking sharks
Diet:	Phytoplankton, zooplankton, tiny fish, fish eggs

Location

The basking shark is found in temperate (10 to 18 °C) and subpolar (below 10 °C) waters of the North and South Atlantic and Pacific Oceans. They swim from the ocean surface to about 570 metres deep.

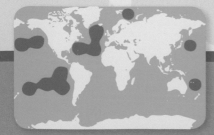

Coastal | *Oceanic*

Sunlit Zone: 0–200 m

Twilight Zone: 200–1000 m

Midnight Zone: 1000–4000 m

Lower Midnight Zone: 4000–6000 m

KRILL

Krill are among the most important animals in the ocean. There are billions of these small, shrimp-like animals. They are eaten by sharks, whales, seals, penguins and seabirds.

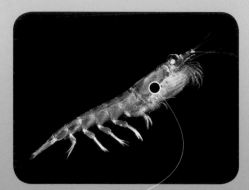

Krill

Living in numbers

Krill live in large groups, called swarms. Up to 30,000 krill can be found in a cubic metre of water. The wriggling swarm confuses hunters.

Squid

Squid catch krill using their long tentacles. Their sharp beaks rip the krill into small pieces for swallowing.

Penguin predator

Krill are an important food for penguins. Chinstrap penguins feed on larger types of krill, while other species of penguin prefer the smaller ones. Penguins, together with whales, seals and other seabirds, eat about 150–300 million tonnes of krill each year.

Whale shark

Whale shark feeding

When they come across clouds of krill, whale sharks hurry to get at the food. They lunge at the krill and churn up the surface of the water as they gulp them into their mouths.

Did you know?

Whale sharks are huge so they have to eat a lot of food to survive. Scientists measured what one young whale shark was eating. It was more than 21 kilograms of food every day.

Basking shark
The basking shark might look like it wants to eat everything in its path, but it is actually harmless to people.

SEAWEEDS

Seaweeds are found in shallow waters close to the coast. They are not proper plants because they do not have leaves, stems or roots, but they do make their own food by photosynthesis. This is when plants take energy from the Sun and create sugars.

Covering rocks

Many seaweeds are found on rocky shores. When they are covered by the tide, their leaf-like fronds float in the water. When the tide goes out, they are left piled up on the rocks until the tide returns.

Seaweed washes up on beaches.

Crested horn shark

The crested horn shark is found off the east coast of Australia. The female lays egg cases which are usually attached to fronds of seaweed. The young sharks hatch from the cases after about eight months.

Harvesting seaweed

People harvest seaweed from the sea. It is eaten as a vegetable in Japan and other countries. Seaweeds are also used as an ingredient in skin cream, shampoo, nail polish, ice cream, beer and paint, and as a fertilizer on soil.

Types of seaweed

There are three main types of seaweed – green, brown and red. Brown seaweed is the most common and is found on rocky beaches. Green seaweed is found only in very shallow water.

KELP FORESTS

Kelp are large seaweeds that grow closely together. Kelp forests, with their fronds gently moving in the water, are magical places where many animals live.

Thin leaves

Kelp have a stalk with long, thin leaves, called fronds, at the top. They are covered in a protective layer of mucus and feel quite tough, but are easily damaged in storms.

Dense growth

Kelp forests are found in fairly shallow water, where the kelp can get enough sunlight to make food. At the surface, they form a thick, tangled mat.

Leopard sharks

Leopard sharks live in shallow waters and are sometimes seen among the kelp forest, usually staying near the bottom.

Did you know?

There are different types of kelp. The giant kelp is the fastest growing of all. It can increase the length of its fronds by up to 60 centimetres every day.

A diver explores kelp forests off the coast of California, North America.

Floating plant
A kelp has a balloon-like float at the base of the fronds. The float is full of air. It keeps the fronds floating near the water's surface, where there is more sunlight.

Kelp eater
Sea urchins eat kelp. In some places, there are too many sea urchins. They eat the young kelp before it has a chance to grow – so the forest disappears.

LEOPARD SHARK

Leopard sharks are one of the most common sharks along the coast of California, North America. They live in shallow waters of the bays and estuaries and occasionally patrol the kelp forest, usually staying near the bottom.

This handsomely marked shark has silvery-bronze skin that is covered with darker oval spots. These markings are what give it its name. The older a leopard shark is, the paler the inside of the spots will be.

Large schools of leopard sharks are a common sight in bays and estuaries. They swim over sandy or muddy flats or rock-strewn areas near kelp beds and reefs. Leopard sharks often follow the tide onto shallow-sloped shorelines to forage for food on the sea bed.

Leopard sharks capture their prey by sucking water in with their mouths. This sucks up the food which is then gripped by the teeth.

Leopard sharks are a target for fishermen who catch them to sell as food. Live leopard sharks are also sold for keeping in aquariums.

Skin
The silvery-bronze skin is patterned with dark ovals that stretch in a neat row across the back.

Profile

Length:	70 to 120 cm (males), 110 to 150 cm (females)
Weight:	Up to 19 kg maximum (males and females)
Order:	Ground sharks
Family:	Hound sharks
Diet:	Bony fish, crabs, clams, shrimps (right), worms

Mouth
The mouth is on the flat underside of its head, and it opens downwards. Perfect for a shark that skims over the sand to pluck up crabs, clams and worms.

Location
The leopard shark is found in shallow temperate (10 to 18 °C) water along the Pacific coast of North America. They swim from the shallows to about 90 metres deep.

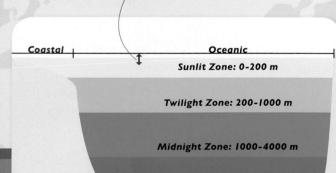

Coastal | Oceanic

Sunlit Zone: 0-200 m

Twilight Zone: 200-1000 m

Midnight Zone: 1000-4000 m

Lower Midnight Zone: 4000-6000 m

KELP FOREST ANIMALS

More than 800 types of animal have been found living in kelp forests. There are shoals of brightly coloured fish, feeding limpets, lurking blue sharks and giant rays.

Garibaldi fish

The bright orange garibaldi fish aggressively defends its nest site in the kelp from all – including divers! The male builds a nest in which the female lays her eggs. He then looks after the eggs until they hatch.

Garibaldi fish nest in the kelp forest.

Eagle ray

The eagle ray has huge wing-like fins that are up to 2 metres wide. It turns on its side to swim between the stalks of the kelp.

Sea otter

Sea otters feed on sea urchins and clams that they find in the kelp forests. Clams have hard shells so otters collect stones, which they use to crack open the shells. They balance the stone on their stomach as they hit the clam shell against it.

Did you know?

Sea otters sometimes wrap themselves in kelp. They use it as an anchor so that they do not drift away while they sleep.

Blue shark

The blue shark is a regular visitor to the kelp forest. It hides in the kelp waiting for prey, such as squid, to pass close by.

A blue shark lurking in the kelp forest.

SEA GRASS

There are underwater sea grass meadows along sheltered coasts. The sea grass shelters large numbers of fish and attracts animals such as turtles, manatees and dolphins. Sharks keep these habitats healthy by intimidating animals that might overgraze on the sea grass.

Underwater grass

Sea grass gets its name from its grass-like appearance, but it is not a proper grass. It is a plant that can grow, rooted in sand, in shallow sea water.

Lobster nursery

Sea grass meadows are nurseries for spiny lobsters. Adult lobsters come here to lay their eggs, out of which hatch baby lobsters. When the lobsters are big enough, they move to nearby swamps and coral reefs.

Manatee

The manatee, or sea cow, looks a bit like a hippopotamus. It has paddle-like front legs to push itself through the water. It uses its large upper lip to graze the sea grass. An adult eats up to 50 kilograms of grass every day.

Did you know?

Scientists in Hawaii found that tiger sharks help to protect sea grass meadows by frightening away the turtles. When the sharks are not around, turtles may eat so much that the meadow is destroyed.

Turtles graze on sea grass meadows.

Sandbar shark

This shark is often found swimming over the muddy or sandy bottom of coastal waters in tropical and temperate oceans around the world. It has a very tall fin on its back. Females can grow to over 2 metres in length.

BALEEN WHALES

Like whale sharks, baleen whales are filter feeders.
But how they filter feed is completely different.
They have comb-like plates hanging from
the roof of their mouth, called baleen plates,
which they use to sieve food from the water.

At more than
30 metres long, the blue
whale is the world's largest
animal. It is a baleen whale.
This giant lives by eating
tiny marine organisms and
can eat up to 40 million
krill a day.

Baleen plates

A whale's baleen plates
are made from keratin –
the same material your
fingernails are made from.
The teeth of these plates are
known as whalebones.

Whale's baleen plate

Shark attack

Baleen whales are
so big that very few
animals in the sea
can hurt them. But
some large sharks
will attack and try
to eat these huge
whales. They target
young calves or
adult whales that
are old or ill, and so
unable to defend
themselves properly.

Water spray is blown up into the air when whales come up to the surface of the water to breathe.

Grooves in this humpback whale's throat allow the throat to expand to four times its usual size when it is feeding.

Blowholes

A blowhole is a whale's nostril, found on top of its head. Whales cannot breathe underwater, so they have to take a deep breath into their lungs before they dive. When they return to the surface, air is forced from their lungs through the blowhole. This sprays water high into the air.

Breaching

Whales sometimes leap out of the water and fall down with a big splash. This is called breaching. Scientists are unsure why they do this. It may be to signal to other whales, or it may be to remove parasites from their skin.

TOOTHED WHALES

Orcas, pilot whales, dolphins and porpoises are toothed whales. Toothed whales usually live together in small groups called pods. They are hunters that feed mostly on fish and squid.

Orcas will surge up onto the beach to catch seals.

Orcas
Orcas (killer whales) behave rather like sharks and can be just as dangerous. Some feed only on fish, but most hunt marine mammals such as sea lions, seals, walruses, and even large whales.

Hunting seals
Some orcas living off the coast of South America have learnt how to surf on to beaches to catch seals. The whales have to be careful not to become stranded on the beach.

A killer whale's top and bottom teeth fit together when it shuts its jaws.

Sharp teeth
Most toothed whales have small, cone-shaped teeth, which are perfect for gripping slippery fish. Orcas have about 50 teeth. Dolphins can have up to 100 teeth.

Dolphin or porpoise?

Dolphins and porpoises look very similar, but a dolphin has a pointed snout and a long, slim body. A porpoise has a rounded fish-like snout and a shorter, rounder body.

A pair of dolphins

Did you know?

Dolphins have been trained by the US Navy to scare off large sharks by butting their gill pouches, but they will not approach a bull shark. This shark is known to attack dolphins in the wild.

NURSE SHARK

The nurse shark is one of the more docile types of shark. It is quite lazy during the day, resting in groups on the bottom of the sea. It starts moving at night, which is when it hunts for food.

Nurse sharks are yellowish tan to dark brown in colour. Young sharks sometimes have small black spots and bands on their skin.

They like warm water and live near the bottom in the shallows, sometimes close to mud or sand flats.

Unlike some sharks, nurse sharks can breathe without having to move through the water. Their respiratory system pumps water over the gills while they rest during the day.

Nurse sharks are bottom feeders. They use their sensitive barbels to search for food in the sand and silt on the ocean floor. They suck up food like a vacuum cleaner, rather than having to grasp it with their teeth.

Barbels
Thin, whisker-like organs on the lower jaw, called barbels, help the shark to find food in the sand and mud of the sea floor.

Profile

Length:	Average 2.1 m (males), average 2.4 m (females)
Weight:	90 to 120 kg (males) and 75 to 105 kg (females)
Order:	Carpet sharks
Family:	Nurse sharks
Diet:	Fish including rays, squid, octopuses, crabs, small invertebrates

Tail fin

An extremely long tail fin makes up about a quarter of the shark's length.

Location

Nurse sharks are found in the tropical (more than 18 °C) waters of the western Atlantic and eastern Pacific Oceans. They swim from the shallows to about 70 metres deep.

Coastal | Oceanic

Sunlit Zone: 0–200 m

Twilight Zone: 200–1000 m

Midnight Zone: 1000–4000 m

Lower Midnight Zone: 4000–6000 m

COASTAL NURSERIES

Many animals visit coastal waters to breed or to have their young. These shallow waters are often sheltered, and there is plenty of food for the young animals.

Hammerhead gathering

Each year, hammerhead sharks gather together in special breeding places. Each male selects a female, and they then mate. After about 10 months, the female swims into shallow water to give birth to her pups.

Hammerhead sharks gathering to breed.

Did you know?

The yearly migration of grey whales from Baja California nurseries to the Arctic feeding grounds and back is a distance of about 20,000 kilometres – the longest journey made by any mammal.

Whale migration

Many whales make regular journeys along the world's coasts. Humpback whales spend the summer in cold waters, where there is plenty of food. They then travel, or migrate, to warmer, shallow water, where the females give birth to their young.

Underwater flier

Manta rays live in the deep sea but give birth in shallow coastal waters, where the young stay for several years. The females are pregnant for about a year before giving birth to one or two pups.

REEF SHARKS

Coral reefs are some of the most colourful places on the planet. They are found in shallow, tropical waters and are home to thousands of different creatures. Several species of reef shark hunt in these waters, preying on fish and other marine animals.

WHERE IN THE WORLD?

Coral reefs are found in warm seas, where the water is shallow and there is plenty of light. Coral will grow only in clean water that is free from pollution.

Reef sharks live in tropical waters and lagoons near coral reefs.

Reef sharks

Reef sharks are the top predators in their part of the oceans. Scientists know that if reef sharks are healthy and present in good numbers, the health of the reef and the fish that live on it must be good too.

Coral is made of polyps. These are tiny animals with tentacles, rather like sea anemones.

Great Barrier Reef

The Great Barrier Reef is the world's largest coral reef. It runs along the northeast coast of Australia and is 2500 kilometres long. Almost 6000 different species of animal live on this reef.

Did you know?

The Great Barrier Reef is the largest structure made by living creatures on Earth. It is so large that it can even be seen from space.

Reefs around the world

Most coral reefs are found in the Indian and Pacific Oceans, the Caribbean and the Red Sea. Corals are not found where there are cold ocean currents or where large rivers flow into the sea.

Greenland

Arctic Ocean

ASIA

EUROPE

NORTH
AMERICA

Atlantic
Ocean

AFRICA

Pacific Ocean

Pacific
Ocean

SOUTH
AMERICA

Indian
Ocean

AUSTRALIA

Coral reefs

Southern Ocean

LIVING REEF

Coral reefs are built by hard corals. These are coral animals that leave behind a stony skeleton when they die. Their skeletons create a habitat in which other animals can live.

Coral polyps

Tiny builders

Reefs are made by groups of tiny coral animals that live together. Each tiny coral animal is called a polyp. A polyp has a tube-like body and a ring of tentacles around its mouth. A reef is made up of millions of polyps all living together in one colony and held together by the stony skeleton.

Living in crevices

Many animals, such as the moray eel, hide in the cracks and crevices on the reef. The moray eel darts out and grabs any small fish that swim too close.

Feather star

Feather stars are related to starfish and live on the coral reef. They have a cup-shaped body and many feathery arms. The arms are covered in a sticky substance that traps small animals as they float by.

Feather star

Snapper fish live on the reef.
Big reef sharks eat fish like this.

Hunting fish

Reef sharks are clever
hunters. They have
found a way of herding
shoals of fish against the
faces of reefs. The fish
cannot swim away, so
are more easy to catch
and eat.

Vase sponges

Sponges

Sponges are animals,
but they do not
move around. Some
sponges grow to
about 2 metres tall.
Others form a flat,
crust-like growth over
the surface of the reef.
There are more than
5000 different types of
sponge. Some of the
largest may be many
hundreds of years old.

REEF SHARKS

Sharks are among the most feared animals on the reef.
Large reef sharks cruise along the reef edge looking for fish,
while smaller sharks hunt shrimps and crabs amongst the corals.

Blacktip reef shark

Blacktip reef sharks are not hunted by
any other animals. This shark hunts in
shallow water and lagoons. It catches
sea snakes as well as fish and octopuses.

Whitetip reef shark

The whitetip reef shark is browny grey
in colour, but has white tips on its fins.
It rests during the day, and hunts for food
at night in the crevices of the coral reef.

Zebra sharks

Zebra sharks live on the reef. Adults have
spots, but when they are young they have
stripes, just like a zebra. Their downward-
pointing mouth is designed to pick up
clams from the sea bed. They also hunt
crabs and small fish.

A whitetip reef shark
resting under a
coral ledge.

Did you know?

Blacktip reef sharks sometimes bite the legs of people who are wading through shallow water. Some experts think it is safer to swim through the shallows, rather than wading.

Blacktip reef sharks have distinctive black markings on the ends of their fins.

Grey reef shark

Grey reef sharks are very aggressive fish. If a diver gets too close, the shark will perform a threat display, warning that it is about to attack. It hunches its back and makes a side-to-side movement in the water.

Caribbean reef shark
This torpedo-shaped shark has become a major tourist attraction in the clear waters of the Caribbean Sea. Some experienced scuba divers go there especially to photograph them.

TYPES OF REEF

There are three types of reef. A fringing reef, formed by corals that follow a coastline, a barrier reef, which grows further away from the land, and a circular reef, called an atoll. Reef sharks live in all three types of reef.

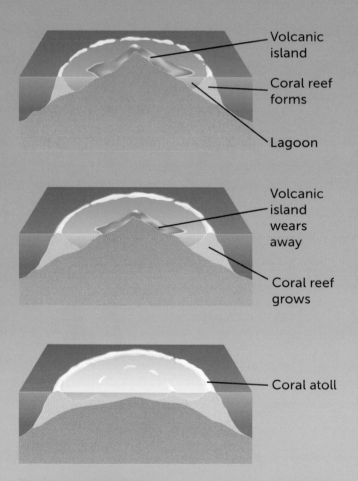

Volcanic island

Coral reef forms

Lagoon

Volcanic island wears away

Coral reef grows

Coral atoll

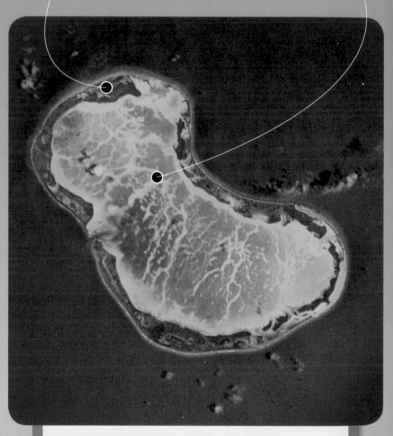

Coral atoll

Lagoon

How an atoll forms

Atolls take millions of years to form. Volcanoes create islands in the oceans. Then coral animals build reefs around the islands. Over a long time, the volcanic islands wear away but the reefs keep growing – leaving behind the atoll rings.

Coral atolls

A coral atoll is a ring of coral reef surrounding an area of shallow water, called a lagoon. The coral reef protects the lagoon from the ocean waves. Most of the world's atolls are found in the Indian and Pacific Oceans.

Did you know?

Whitetip and grey reef
sharks prefer clear water.
Whitetip reef sharks like
the water in lagoons, and
grey reef sharks prefer the
deeper waters off
the reef edge.

New coral

Coral polyps like to grow on
something hard. They will even
make their home on the remains
of a sunken ship. Eventually
the wreck becomes a new
habitat for sharks, smaller fish
and other marine animals.

Coral sand

Waves batter against the coral reef,
and the reef gradually wears away.
The tiny particles of reef are washed
up on the shore as sand, eventually
creating beautiful tropical beaches.

A beach with
fine coral sand.

BLACKTIP REEF SHARK

Fast-swimming and active, the blacktip reef shark is one of the three most common sharks inhabiting coral reefs in the tropical waters of the Indian Ocean and the western and central Pacific Ocean. It is mostly found in shallow inshore waters.

These streamlined sharks are brownish-grey on their upper surfaces and white underneath.

They are fast and active hunters, pursuing small fish and invertebrates back and forth around the reef. The patch of water in which they hunt is quite small in size and they do not stray far from these home waters, often staying in the same area for years at a time. Most blacktip reef sharks are found near rocky ledges and sandy flats, though they have also been known to swim into brackish (partly salty) water and even into fresh water near the sea.

This shark is quite timid and does not pose a serious threat to humans. However, it has been known to bite people that come close when swimming, and particularly when wading, in shallow water.

Head
The snout is short and blunt, the eyes are oval and the mouth is filled with narrow saw-edged teeth.

Fins
All the fins have black or dark brown tips. This is highlighted on the dorsal fin, which has a light band beneath it.

Profile

Length:	1.6 to 1.8 m (males and females)
Weight:	Up to 14 kg maximum (males and females)
Order:	Ground sharks
Family:	Requiem sharks
Diet:	Small fish, squid, shrimps, octopuses (right)

Tail
A sickle-shaped tail fin built for speed propels the blacktip reef shark through the water.

Location
Blacktip reef sharks are found in the shallow tropical (more than 18 °C) waters of the Indo-Pacific Oceans and the eastern Mediterranean Sea. They swim from the shallows to about 70 metres deep.

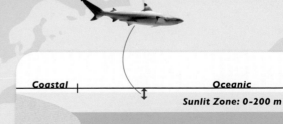

Coastal	Oceanic
	Sunlit Zone: 0–200 m
	Twilight Zone: 200–1000 m
	Midnight Zone: 1000–4000 m
	Lower Midnight Zone: 4000–6000 m

HARD CORALS

Hard corals are those with limestone skeletons. There are many different species of hard coral, each forming an interesting shape on the reef.

Table coral

Table coral is a fast-growing, spreading coral that forms a flat, table-like shape. It grows to several metres across and is made up of lots of short branches.

Mushroom coral

The mushroom coral is round or oval in shape. It can be flat or domed and is usually about 50 centimetres across. Most corals are made up of many polyps, but this type has just one large one.

Table coral

Black coral

Brain coral is shaped like a ball
with furrows on its surface.

Brain coral

Brain coral gets its name
from the way it looks like
the folded surface of a real
brain. These corals
grow up to 1.8 metres tall,
and are strong enough to
survive in rough seas.

Black coral

Black corals are found
in deeper water, where
there is less light. They are
branching corals, which
look a bit like bushes with
little branches. The skeleton
is black but the polyps are
white, yellow or orange.

Did you know?

Black coral is in danger
of dying out because too
much has been collected.
It is made into jewellery.
Some divers risk diving very
deep to gather black coral
that they can sell.

CARIBBEAN REEF SHARK

The Caribbean reef shark is one of the most common sharks in the Caribbean. It is most active at night when it hunts for fish and invertebrates to eat.

A Caribbean reef shark has the muscular, streamlined shape that is typical of requiem sharks. It has a dark grey to grey-brown back, and white to light yellow stomach.

Caribbean reef sharks live near coral reefs and ocean bottoms near the continental and island shelves. They prefer shallow waters with a maximum depth of 30 metres. They are often found on the outer edges of coral reefs and sometimes even lying motionless on the ocean floor.

They feed mainly on small fish, which they grasp in the corner of the mouth. They use a sudden sideways snap of the jaws.

Some people stage shark feeds for tourists. Critics claim that this changes the natural balance of the food chain – the sharks may start to see humans as reliable sources of food, increasing the chances of a shark attack on humans.

Fins
The tips of the lower fins are dark, as are the rear edges of the large tail fin.

Profile

Length:	1.5 to 1.7 m (males) and up to 3 m (females)
Weight:	Up to 70 kg maximum (males and females)
Order:	Ground sharks
Family:	Requiem sharks
Diet:	Fish including rays, invertebrates such as octopuses and squid

Eyes

Large and circular eyes, with protective third eyelids that can be drawn across the eyes as protection.

Location

Caribbean reef sharks are found in the shallow tropical (more than 18 °C) waters of the western Atlantic Ocean down to northern Brazil. These streamlined sharks swim from the shallows to about 30 metres deep.

Coastal | *Oceanic*

Sunlit Zone: 0–200 m

Twilight Zone: 200–1000 m

Midnight Zone: 1000–4000 m

Lower Midnight Zone: 4000–6000 m

SOFT CORALS

Soft corals come in a wide range of colours, such as red, yellow, orange and purple. Soft corals are those that do not have a hard skeleton.

Did you know?

Soft coral is known as a flower animal because it can take on many different shapes and colours. The bright colours are warning signs to fish that the coral is poisonous.

Underwater fans
Fan corals form beautiful fan shapes, up to 3 metres across, which move gently in the currents. Each fan has a flexible stem fixing it firmly to the rocks.

Fan corals are also called sea fans.

Feeding corals
Coral polyps feed by extending their tentacles into the water to catch small animals. The tentacles are covered in stinging cells, which they use to kill their prey and to defend themselves.

Whip coral
Whip corals look a bit like long drinking straws. They bend in the ocean currents, catching plankton to eat, but do not get damaged.

Yellow finger gorgonian coral.

Whip coral has long, whip-like branches covered in tiny polyps.

Fire coral

Fire corals have a powerful sting. This protects the polyps from coral-eating fish. Fire corals are often found on the edge of the reef as they can survive in rough water.

LIVING TOGETHER

Animals live closely together on the reef. Some depend on others for a home, to stay clean or for protection from predators.

Keeping a balance

Healthy coral reefs need sharks. Without sharks, large reef fish seriously reduce the numbers of algae-eating fish. The coral then suffers because too much algae on a reef kills it.

Caribbean reef shark

Cleaning station

Fish have difficulty removing the tiny parasites that live on their body, so they visit 'cleaning stations' on the reef. Here, small fish and cleaner shrimps remove and eat the parasites for them.

Clown fish

Decorator crabs attach sponges and seaweeds to their shell. These living decorations help to disguise the crab from predators.

Living with stings

Anemones are covered in sting cells. Most animals stay away, but not the clown fish. It lives in the safety of the tentacles as it is covered with a slimy mucus that protects it from the stings.

A coral grouper fish is cleaned by cleaner shrimps.

Living camouflage

The hermit crab protects its soft body by living inside an empty shell. Anemones have attached themselves to this hermit crab's shell. The anemones provide the crab with camouflage and protection and, in return, the crab helps the anemones to find food.

Wash and brush-up

The coral grouper fish opens its mouth so that a cleaner shrimp can remove parasites from every nook and cranny. The shrimp gets a meal, and the fish is rid of parasites.

EATING CORAL

Coral is an important source of food for many reef animals, including turtles, starfish, snails and lots of fish. These eat the coral polyps themselves and also tiny organisms that live within the reef.

Parrot fish

The parrot fish uses its large, beak-like teeth to bite off lumps of coral covered in algae, crunching them into small pieces. Much of the coral passes through its gut and ends up as sand on a beach!

The parrot fish gets its name from its teeth which look like a parrot's beak.

Did you know?

Overfishing of sharks is causing 'desertification' of coral reefs. This is when the coral dies and turns white. Without sharks, the balance of the reef is changed. Huge algae blooms can grow that stifle the coral.

Hawksbill turtle

This turtle has a pointed beak like that of a bird. It is perfect for reaching into crevices on the reef to grasp sponges, which are its favourite food.

Butterfly fish

Butterfly fish have a flat body and a long, thin snout. They are the perfect shape to pick up small animals from inside coral crevices. Butterfly fish have colourful patterns – just like butterflies!

Hawksbill turtle

Reef devourer

The large crown-of-thorns starfish has a huge appetite for coral. It has up to 18 arms and is covered with poisonous spines. At night, it crawls on to coral and empties its stomach contents. The digestive juices turn the coral into a liquid, which the starfish then sucks up.

One crown-of-thorns starfish can eat up to 13 square metres of coral in a year.

Grey reef shark

The grey reef shark is often found in fairly shallow
water around reefs in the tropical seas of the Indian
Ocean and western and central Pacific Ocean. They
grow to around 2 metres long and feed mainly on
fish and molluscs, such as squid and octopuses.

HUNTERS ON THE REEF

Sharks are not the only predators on the reef. Barracuda, octopuses and lion fish are also attracted to the thousands of fish and small animals living on the reef.

Reef sharks are apex predators – they are not preyed upon by other predators.

Barracuda

The barracuda has powerful jaws, knife-like teeth and a long body. It hangs in the water without moving, then darts forwards to grab prey with a burst of speed.

Lion fish

This is a dangerous fish – its spines are tipped with poison. Lion fish trap prey using their large, spiny fins – and then swallow it whole.

Lion fish

Reef octopus

The reef octopus hides in holes with just its legs sticking out. It grabs its prey of fish or clams with its suckers and pulls it towards its mouth. The octopus then uses its powerful beak to crush its meal.

WHITETIP REEF SHARK

One of the most common sharks found around coral reefs in the Indian and Pacific Oceans, the whitetip reef shark is typically found on or near the bottom in clear water.

During the day, whitetip reef sharks spend much of their time resting inside caves or even out in the open, lying on the sea bed. Unlike other requiem sharks, which must constantly swim to breathe, the whitetip can lie still on the bottom without fear of drowning, as it can pump water over its gills.

At night, they start to hunt. Their bodies are ideal for wriggling their way into gaps in the reef in pursuit of fish. They sometimes break off bits of the coral in their eagerness to snatch the prey. Their target fish are beyond the reach of other species of shark that feed in open water. For this reason whitetips are able to live alongside other species of reef shark without competing for the same sources of food.

Body
A long, thin body, perfect for worming its way into small cracks in the reef.

Head
The head is short but broad, with whisker-like skin flaps beside the nostrils, called barbels.

Profile

Length:	1.1 to 1.6 m (males and females)
Weight:	Up to 18 kg maximum (males and females)
Order:	Ground sharks
Family:	Requiem sharks
Diet:	Fish, octopuses, crabs, spiny lobsters (right)

Fins
Prominent white tips on the first dorsal fin and the tail fin give the whitetip reef shark its name.

Location
Whitetip reef sharks are found in the shallow tropical and subtropical (more than 18 °C) waters of the Indo-Pacific Oceans and along the western coast of Central America. They swim from the shallows to about 40 metres deep.

Coastal | Oceanic

Sunlit Zone: 0-200 m

Twilight Zone: 200-1000 m

Midnight Zone: 1000-4000 m

Lower Midnight Zone: 4000-6000 m

REEF DEFENCE

Reef animals protect themselves from predators, such as sharks, in different ways. Some use body armour or poisons to defend themselves. Others rely on camouflage to keep them hidden on the reef.

Hiding in coral

Corals make great hiding places for the creatures that live on them. To escape from the many kinds of predators that are trying to eat them, they can hide in the thousands of cracks and crevices that are part of the reef structure.

Body armour

Seahorses use body armour to defend themselves. The tough armour gives them good protection, but makes swimming more difficult. They stay still much of the time, relying on their camouflage to hide them from hungry hunters.

Frog camouflage

Frog fish look more like a piece of coral or sponge than a fish. By keeping perfectly still, they blend in with the reef and are difficult for predators to spot.

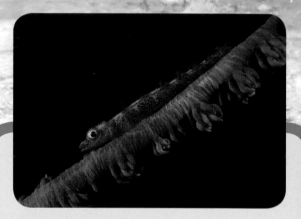

Hide and seek

Tiny animals, such as this small goby, hide from their predators on and among the coral branches. The smallest gobies are less than 1 centimetre long.

Did you know?

The reef stonefish is one of the most poisonous fish in the world. It has 13 spines, which inject poison into anything that touches them.

Spiny defence

The cowfish's spiky body armour, with long spines over each eye, gives it an unusual appearance. If the cowfish is attacked, it can also release a poison into the water from its skin.

Reef stonefish look like a lump of rock or coral. This is brilliant camouflage.

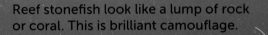

Blacktip reef shark

Blacktips like to stay in a fairly small area of water. They spend most of the time swimming back and forth along the edges of a reef looking for their prey, which is mainly small fish.

OUT AT NIGHT

The reef is active at night because many of the animals are nocturnal. They hide during the day in caves and crevices, then come out to feed in the safety of the dark.

Cardinal fish

Whitetip reef shark

This shark mostly rests during the day, often lying with other whitetips. It becomes active at night when it hunts for food. It likes prey that live on the sea bed in caves and crevices in the reef, especially octopuses, crabs, lobsters, fish and eels.

Cardinal fish

The female cardinal fish lays her eggs in the water, where they are fertilized by the male. The male then collects them in his mouth and cares for them until they hatch. He releases the young fish in the safety of darkness.

Did you know?

The whitetip reef shark's thick skin protects it from getting cuts and grazes when bumping into the sharp coral.

Safety in numbers

Snappers are seen at night swimming around in small groups. They hunt crabs, shrimps, worms and fish that live on sandy sea beds near reefs.

Whitetip reef shark

Squirrel fish

Squirrel fish have extra-large eyes to help them see in low light conditions. The fish hide in caves and wrecked ships by day, and come out at night to feed on plankton.

REEF MOLLUSCS

Molluscs are a group of animals that include snails, clams and squid. Most molluscs have a muscular 'foot', which they use to move around.

Giant clam

The giant clam is a bivalve – a snail with two shells that are hinged together. Clams stay in one place on the reef, sucking water into their body and filtering out plankton. Their colour comes from algae, which live in their cells and provide the clams with food.

Nudibranch

Nudibranches are soft-bodied sea slugs that have no shell. Without a shell for protection, they use poison to defend themselves against predators. They are brightly coloured to warn other animals that they are poisonous.

Nudibranches live on the sea bed.

The giant clam can open and close the two halves of its shell.

Did you know?

The largest giant clams grow to more than a metre across, weigh more than 200 kilogrammes and can live for up to 100 years.

Mollusc hunter

The zebra shark hunts mainly at night. It feeds on molluscs that live on the sea bed. It will also eat crustaceans, small fish and even sea snakes. These sharks swim rather like eels do, waving their body and tail from side to side to move through the water. Adults can grow to around 2.5 metres long.

Coral eaters

These flamingo tongue snails are coral eaters. As they crawl over the coral, their feet release digestive juices. The juices dissolve the polyps, and the snails absorb the nutrients through their foot.

Shell protection

A heavy shell, such as this helmet shell, protects the soft body of a snail. When threatened, the snail retreats into its shell.

The shell of a tongue snail is white. The spots are on a thin layer that covers the shell.

OCEAN SHARKS

Stretching beyond the coastal waters is the vast open ocean. It covers thousands of square kilometres of the Earth's surface and extends down for thousands of metres. Many different marine animals live in these huge stretches of water, including some of the strangest-looking, fiercest and most amazing sharks of all.

SURFACE WATERS

The open oceans are home to fewer animals than coral reefs and coastal waters. Most animals that do live here are found in the surface layer, which is the top 200 metres.

Light in the water
The ocean's surface is lit by sunlight. The top 30 metres is brightly lit, but it gets darker as you go deeper. By 200 metres, all sunlight has gone and the water looks blue-black.

Did you know?

During storms at sea, it is not unusual for waves to reach more than 30 metres in height. That is as tall as a 10-storey building!

Surface waves
When the wind blows over the surface of the ocean it creates waves. As the waves grow larger they are moved along by the wind, and this helps to mix up the water.

Counter-shading

Many sharks have dark backs and white stomachs. This is called counter-shading. From above, their dark backs blend with the depths of the water below. From below, their light stomachs blend with the sunlight coming from above.

The wind blowing over the surface of the sea pushes along wind-powered boats, such as this yacht.

Flying fish

The flying fish has an unusual way of escaping predators. When threatened, it swims straight at the surface of the water and flies into the air, using its fins like wings. It can glide above the surface for up to 100 metres.

FLOATING LIFE

The surface layer is home to many floating animals, both large and small.
These are carried across the ocean by the currents and waves.

Food source

The tiny plants and animals that float near the surface attract whales and sharks that eat them. The whales and sharks migrate long distances to follow this source of food.

Tiny hunters

The larvae of squid and fish are found in the surface layer, where they drift in the currents. These tiny larvae hunt even smaller animals, such as copepods and amphipods.

Did you know?

Most oceanic sharks must keep swimming forwards in order to force seawater through their open mouths and over their gills to breathe – otherwise they would suffocate.

Floating stings

The Portuguese man-of-war looks like a jellyfish but it is a siphonophore. One polyp floats above the surface to catch the wind. Others form hanging tentacles to trap food.

Siphonophores

Siphonophores are formed from a colony of individual polyps – each with a different job to do. Their long, stinging tentacles dangle in the water to catch fish and shrimps.

After making deep dives, whale sharks usually return to the surface to warm up.

WHALE SHARK

This is a true giant – the largest fish in the ocean. Despite its name it is not a whale, but a gigantic shark that cruises slowly through the sea sucking in vast amounts of water as it filter-feeds.

The whale shark has distinctive light-yellow markings (random stripes and spots) dotted across its skin. Its skin can be up to 10 centimetres thick. The underlying colour is usually dark grey, blue or brown. Three large ridges run down each side of its body.

These sharks live in warm water, normally out in the open sea, although they do also come fairly close to shore. They are usually solitary feeders swimming near the surface, where they scoop up vast amounts of plankton and small fish in their huge mouths. These are sieved out from the water using a technique called filter feeding.

Whale sharks are quite harmless to humans. They are not worried by scuba divers coming close to them in the water.

Mouth
A huge gaping mouth to hoover up plankton and small fish.

Profile

Length:	6 to 12 m (males and females)
Weight:	Typically around 15 tonnes (males and females), 20 tonnes maximum
Order:	Carpet sharks
Family:	Whale sharks
Diet:	Plankton (right), small fish, crustaceans

Gill slits

Large bristly gill rakers, behind each gill slit, filter particles of food from the water.

Location

Whale sharks are found worldwide in tropical (more than 18 °C) and warm temperate (10 °C to 18 °C) waters. They swim from the surface to 700 metres deep.

Coastal	Oceanic
	Sunlit Zone: 0–200 m
	Twilight Zone: 200–1000 m
	Midnight Zone: 1000–4000 m
	Lower Midnight Zone: 4000–6000 m

JELLYFISH

Few marine animals will try to eat jellyfish because their sting is so painful. But some big fish, including tiger sharks, do eat them. They can swallow them without being hurt by the stings.

Jellyfish are not actually fish – they are related to corals and sea anemones. They are invertebrates with a soft, bell-shaped body with tentacles hanging beneath the bell. Each tentacle is covered in cells that can sting or kill other creatures.

Some jellyfish are so poisonous that they are a danger to humans. Each year more people are killed by jellyfish than by great white sharks.

Most jellyfish float in the water and are carried around by currents. Some can swim very slowly by squeezing water in and out of their bell – which looks a bit like an umbrella opening and closing. This movement sends pulses of water out of the back of the jellyfish, causing it to move forwards.

Mauve stinger jellyfish are found mainly in warm waters in the open ocean.

Lion's mane

The largest jellyfish is the lion's mane. Its bell is more than a metre across and the tentacles are many metres long. They eat almost anything that bumps into their tentacles.

Sea nettles

Sea nettles are a small type of jellyfish. Each year, in some parts of the world, swarms of sea nettles gather together to lay eggs. Sea nettles can sting, so people and marine animals stay away from these areas.

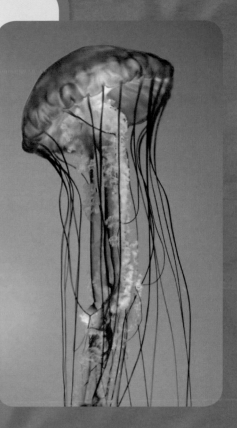

Did you know?

Jellyfish have been around for more than 650 million years, which means that they are older than both dinosaurs and sharks.

SHOALS OF FISH

Many fish live together in groups called shoals. Some shoals contain just a few fish but, when shoals join together, a huge shoal of hundreds of thousands of fish may form.

Living in groups

Fish are safer in large groups. A shoal of fish confuses hunters by darting around in different directions. The fish use their senses to make sure that they do not bump into each other.

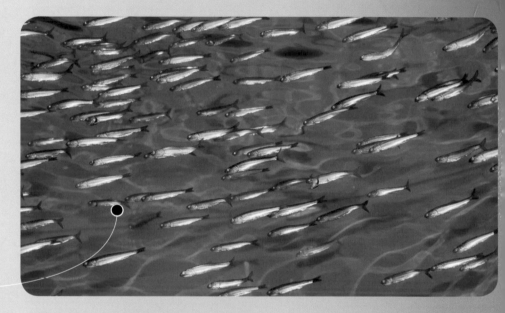

Sardines form huge shoals that attract hunters such as sharks, dolphins and swordfish.

Working as a team

Sharks sometimes work together to hunt shoals of fish. They scare the fish into a tight ball, and then attack the trapped prey.

Bigeye jacks

These fish are powerful hunters with large eyes and a forked tail. They patrol the oceans in large shoals seeking out smaller fish, which they catch in their large jaws. These fish can grow up to 1 metre long.

A shoal of fish moves away from an approaching diver.

Did you know?

During the 1970s, enormous herring shoals of more than three billion fish were thought to exist in the North Atlantic Ocean.

BLUE SHARK

The blue shark is a long-distance traveller. It swims hundreds of kilometres every year, searching for food or to mate.

The blue shark has a bright blue back and a white stomach – these colours help to hide it in the ocean. Viewed from above, the deep blue blends with the murky waters; viewed from below, the white helps the shark to blend in with the light coming from above.

These large sharks hunt with their mouths wide open, trapping small fish, such as sardines, in their jaws. They also feed on squid and other invertebrates, such as octopuses and cuttlefish.

Blue sharks are slow swimmers but can move very quickly when attacking their prey. They travel long distances in their widespread habitat. One blue shark made a trip over 6437 kilometres from New York to Brazil!

Eyes
Large eyes are protected by a transparent third eyelid which the shark can flick over the eyeball when it is hunting.

Tail
A long tail provides swimming power as the tail moves side-to-side.

Pectoral fins
Long pectoral fins – the same length as the distance between the tip of the snout and the last gill slit.

Profile

Length:	1.8–2.8 m long (males), 2.2–3.3 m long (females)
Weight:	27–55 kg (males), 93–182 kg (females)
Order:	Ground sharks
Family:	Requiem sharks
Diet:	Bony fish, squid and other invertebrates

Teeth
Teeth with jagged edges ensure a better grip on squid and other slimy sea creatures with slippery bodies.

Location

Blue sharks are found worldwide in temperate (10 to 18 °C) waters and at lower depths in tropical (more than 18 °C) waters. They swim from the surface to about 350 metres deep.

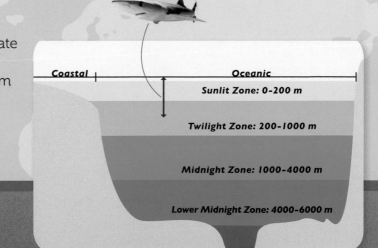

Coastal | Oceanic

Sunlit Zone: 0-200 m

Twilight Zone: 200-1000 m

Midnight Zone: 1000-4000 m

Lower Midnight Zone: 4000-6000 m

SQUID

Squid are an important link in the ocean food chain. It is a hunter of smaller animals, such as krill and fish, and is itself the prey of hunters such as sharks, swordfish and dolphins.

A squid has eight arms and two longer tentacles. When it gets close to its prey, it shoots out its long tentacles to grab the animal and pull it into its mouth.

To move along, a squid draws water into its body and then forces it out through a funnel on its belly. This creates a powerful jet of water that pushes the squid backwards through the water. It can also move its fins to help it swim along.

Did you know?

Large squid can move at 30 kilometres per hour, faster than many ships can travel. But they can only go this fast in short bursts, when chasing food or escaping from a predator.

This squid has caught a fish in its tentacles.

Squid have small suckers that cover the underside of the arms.

Large eye
Squid have large eyes that are very similar to human eyes, with a pupil and a lens. They rely on their sight to find prey.

Colourful messages

Squid can change the colour of their skin. They can blend into the background or change colour to confuse a predator. Their colour reflects their mood too. Angry squid are often red. This squid is bioluminescent – it gives off an eerie glow in the dark.

GREAT HAMMERHEAD SHARK

There are nine species of hammerhead sharks and the great hammerhead is the biggest of them. The shape of their head is unique.

Great hammerhead sharks are grey-brown to olive green on top with an off-white underside.

No-one knows for sure why their head has such a strange shape. Scientists think that the extra distance between its eyes gives the shark a huge field of vision both above and below. Masses of special sensors on the underside of the 'hammer' may allow it to detect the presence of stingrays when they are lying buried in the sand on the bottom. Some hammerheads have even been seen to pin a stingray to the seafloor with their heads while they take a bite out of its wings to stop it escaping.

Great hammerheads migrate – they head to warmer waters during the winter and then return to their normal feeding grounds in the summer.

Dorsal fin
A tall and pointed dorsal fin helps to stabilize the shark when it is turning quickly in the water as it hunts for prey.

Head
The head is shaped like a flattened hammer with the eyes set at the edges.

Tail

A tall tail fin made up of a large upper section, called a lobe, and smaller lower section, propels the shark through the water.

Profile

Length:	4 to 6 m (males and females)
Weight:	230 to 450 kg (males and females)
Order:	Ground sharks
Family:	Hammerhead sharks
Diet:	Fish, including rays (below) and other sharks, squid, octopuses, crustaceans

Location

Great hammerheads are found worldwide in tropical and subtropical (more than 18 °C) waters. They swim from the surface to about 80 metres deep.

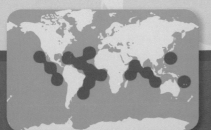

Coastal	Oceanic
	Sunlit Zone: 0–200 m
	Twilight Zone: 200–1000 m
	Midnight Zone: 1000–4000 m
	Lower Midnight Zone: 4000–6000 m

OCEAN HUNTERS

Large hunting fish, such as sharks, swordfish, sailfish and marlin, are at the top of the ocean food chain. These fearsome fish are designed for hunting.

Marlin

The marlin is related to the tuna and swordfish. It is a large fish with a spear-like snout. It hunts alone, swimming in the surface waters of the ocean in search of fish and squid.

Sailfish

These fish have a large, sail-like fin along their back. They use it to gather together groups of fish and squid, which they then eat. Sailfish can fold back the fin to create a sleek, streamlined shape for swimming.

Did you know?

Mako sharks are very strong and fierce. Some makos have been known to leap into a fishing boat to try to attack the fisherman.

Mako sharks can leap clear out of the water when they are swimming really fast.

Mako shark

The mako is a muscular fish with a tail fin shaped for speed. It can swim at up to 50 kilometres an hour. It has sharp teeth, which it uses to grip slippery prey such as tuna and mackerel.

Swordfish

The swordfish is named after its long, sword-like snout. It does not spear its prey, but moves its 'sword' from side to side to slice it up. It swims alone and is often seen leaping out of the water.

Scalloped hammerhead shark
This shark's name comes from the 'scallops' along the front edge of its hammer. These are missing on other hammerhead sharks. The eyes and nostrils are at the sides of the hammer.

OCEAN GIANTS

Sharks share the oceans with other giant creatures, such as enormous whales, disc-shaped sunfish and winged manta rays.

Oceanic whitetip shark

The oceanic whitetip shark grows to about 2 metres long. It swims just below the surface, but sometimes sticks its nose out of the water to sniff the air in search of food.

An oceanic whitetip shark with pilot fish swimming alongside it.

Manta ray

A manta ray usually swims slowly through the ocean, but when threatened by predators, such as sharks, it leaps out of the water in an attempt to escape.

Humpback whale

The humpback whale can grow up to 16 metres long (the same length as a bus) and weigh approximately 36,000 kilograms.

Sunfish

The sunfish has an unusual shape – it is almost circular when seen from the side, with fins sticking out of the top and bottom of its body. Sunfish feed on jellyfish, and can weigh more than 2000 kilograms.

SILKY SHARK

This is one of the most common sharks in the open ocean. There are tens of millions of these slim, agile predators living in tropical waters around the world.

The back of the silky shark ranges in colour from dark brown to a blue-grey. The underside is generally white and the lower fins can have dark tips on their underside.

This shark usually hunts on it own and generally attacks fish swimming in open water. It is particularly attracted to tuna and is often seen trailing behind shoals of these fish. Sometimes, when there are lots of fish in the water, silky sharks will hunt together in a pack. They 'herd' the shoal towards the surface. Then they slice into the shoal with their mouths open, to trap them in their jaws.

Silky sharks can act aggressively towards humans, but as they are normally found out in the open ocean, they do not often come into contact with divers.

Skin
The skin is smooth to the touch, unlike the skin of other species of sharks which is rough.

Pectoral fin
Long and curved pectoral fins give the shark lift as it swims through the water.

Dorsal fin
A short, rounded dorsal fin helps the silky shark balance.

Profile

Length:	1.8 to 2.1 m (males), 2.1 to 2.3 m (females)
Weight:	175 to 300 kg (males and females), 346 kg maximum
Order:	Ground sharks
Family:	Requiem sharks
Diet:	Fish (right), squid, crustaceans

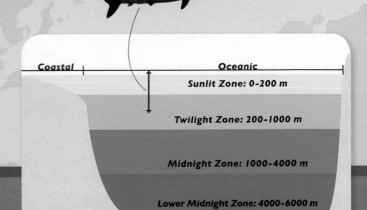

Location

Silky sharks are found worldwide in tropical and subtropical waters, usually at a temperature of 23 °C or more. They swim from around 18 metres to about 500 metres deep.

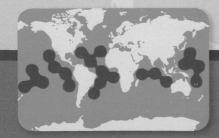

Coastal	Oceanic
	Sunlit Zone: 0-200 m
	Twilight Zone: 200-1000 m
	Midnight Zone: 1000-4000 m
	Lower Midnight Zone: 4000-6000 m

OCEAN TURTLES

Many sharks eat turtles, including tiger sharks, great white sharks, short-finned mako sharks, bull sharks and oceanic whitetip sharks.

Turtles make long journeys across the oceans in search of food. They return to the beach where they were born to lay their eggs. All sea turtles give birth by laying eggs. The female will bury between 50 and 200 eggs (depending on the species) in the sand. After around 60 days, baby turtles hatch out of the eggs. They dig their way out of the sand and instinctively make for the sea.

Turtles spend the first few years of their life in the open ocean. They feed on jellyfish and other animals there before returning to coastal waters to mate.

Green turtles

Green turtles are expert swimmers with a smooth, streamlined shell and flippers. They are the largest hard-shelled turtle in the ocean. They grow to a metre across, and weigh 200 kilograms or more. Baby green turtles are meat eaters, but adults feed on sea grass.

Turtles have flat flippers to help them swim.

Sharks can get rid of material in their stomachs that they cannot digest, like the turtle's shell, by turning their stomach inside out. The shell is vomited out of the mouth.

All turtles are toothless. Instead of teeth, they use their beak to crush coral and crabs, or graze on sea grass.

Hawksbill turtles

This rare turtle gets its name from the bird-like shape of its head. It spends as long as 20 years at sea before it is ready to breed. Sadly, it is killed for its attractive shell, which is used to make jewellery and ornaments.

OCEANIC WHITETIP SHARK

Oceanic whitetip sharks live in the open ocean. They often follow ships hoping to pick up scraps of food thrown overboard. For this reason, ancient sailors used to call them 'sea dogs'.

The upper surface of the oceanic whitetip shark's body varies from greyish-bronze to brown in colour, depending upon where it is in the world. The underside is whitish, sometimes with a yellow tinge.

The oceanic whitetip usually hunts alone and is quite slow-moving. It tends to cruise in the open ocean quite near to the surface. It covers vast stretches of empty water scanning for food. However, when it gets near its prey – usually fish or invertebrates – it can put on sudden bursts of speed.

When an oceanic whitetip senses the smell of blood in the water, it may go into a feeding frenzy, swimming about wildly and biting anything that comes near.

Oceanic whitetips are dangerous to humans because of their predatory nature. During the Second World War they caused the deaths of many sailors and airmen who found themselves in the water after their ships were sunk or their aircraft were shot down.

Teeth
Sharp triangular upper teeth and smaller pointed lower teeth are ideal for holding and tearing the shark's prey.

Dorsal fins
This shark has a big, rounded first fin on its back.

Profile

Length:	1.7 to 1.9 m (males), 1.8 to 2 m (females)
Weight:	35 to 70 kg (males and females), 167 kg maximum
Order:	Ground sharks
Family:	Requiem sharks
Diet:	Fish, squid and other molluscs, sea turtles, crustaceans

Pectoral fins
Long, paddle-like fins are set low behind the gill slits. All the large fins have white tips.

Location
Oceanic whitetip sharks are found worldwide in tropical waters, usually at a temperature between 20 and 28 °C. They swim from the surface to about 150 metres deep.

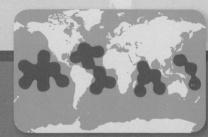

Coastal   Oceanic

Sunlit Zone: 0-200 m

Twilight Zone: 200-1000 m

Midnight Zone: 1000-4000 m

Lower Midnight Zone: 4000-6000 m

DOLPHINS

Large species of sharks, such as the great white shark, will eat dolphins, but most sharks do not prey on them. The dolphin is one of the most intelligent animals in the ocean. This playful marine mammal uses sound to find its prey, and lives in groups.

Living together

Dolphins live together in groups called pods. A pod usually contains about 10 to 12 dolphins, but super pods of thousands of dolphins are formed when pods join up for a short period. This happens when food is found in great quantities.

Dolphins are athletic swimmers and love to play together.

Hunting with sound

Dolphins use sound to find their prey. This is called echolocation. They make whistling and clicking sounds, which travel through the water. These sound waves bounce off any prey in the water, creating echoes that the dolphins can hear. The echoes tell the dolphin the shape, size and location of their prey.

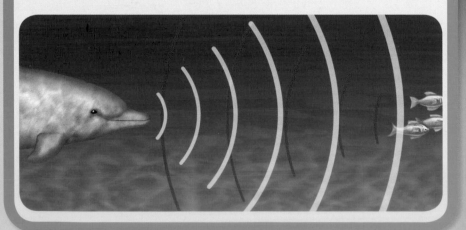

Did you know?

In 2004, dolphins saved the lives of four swimmers who were threatened by a great white shark off the coast of New Zealand. The dolphins swam in circles around the people until the shark swam away.

Leaping dolphins

The acrobatic dolphin moves its powerful tail up and down to build up enough speed to jump out of the water. Dolphins often leap into the air while chasing fish to eat. Sometimes they even play chase with other dolphins.

Looking after baby

A female dolphin gives birth to her baby, or calf, underwater. The mother pushes her calf to the surface so it can take its first breath. The calf feeds on its mother's milk for about a year.

Oceanic whitetip shark
The large fins on this ocean shark have made it
a target for fishermen who supply shark fins to the
food industry. These are turned into shark's fin soup.
Unfortunately, this dish is very popular and whitetip
numbers have fallen dramatically.

SARGASSO SEA

The Sargasso Sea is a huge area of floating seaweed in the Atlantic Ocean. It is home to many animals — some stay all year, but others, like porbeagle sharks, are just visitors.

Sargassum weed

Thick mats of sargassum weed cover much of the Sargasso Sea. This weed is free-floating, not attached to rocks or the sea bed. Turtles and fish hide among the mats, while crabs and small shrimps cling to the weed.

Eels

Adult eels swim to the Sargasso Sea to lay their eggs. The young eels hatch. They then make their way back to North America and Europe.

Location

The Sargasso Sea covers an area of about 3 million square kilometres. It is an area with slow ocean currents surrounded by fast-moving currents that circulate around the Sargasso Sea in a clockwise direction.

NORTH AMERICA

SOUTH AMERICA

EUROPE

Atlantic Ocean

Sargasso Sea

AFRICA

Did you know?

The vast Sargasso Sea is the only sea in the world that does not have a coastline. Instead it is bordered by fast-moving water.

Small air sacs keep the sargassum weed afloat.

Porbeagle sharks

Female porbeagle sharks migrate south to the Sargasso Sea to give birth to their pups. The young pups and the adult sharks then make their way back to the cooler North Atlantic, where they spend most of the year.

MOVING UP AND DOWN

During the day, the brightly lit surface waters are virtually empty of small animals. Most dive to the safety of the darker water below. They return to feed under the cover of darkness.

Night-time travellers

This daily movement is only a few hundred metres, but for tiny animals, such as shrimps and copepods, it is a long journey. It is the only way to feed in safety.

Shrimp

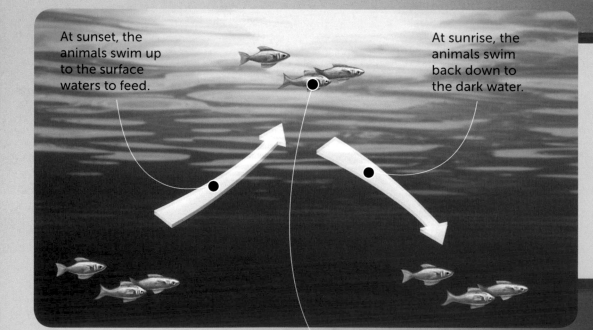

At sunset, the animals swim up to the surface waters to feed.

At sunrise, the animals swim back down to the dark water.

Mass migration

Most types of plankton and some types of plankton-eating fish migrate up and down, including krill, herring and mackerel.

At night, the animals feed on plankton.

Lantern fish

Lantern fish travel the greatest distances each day. During daylight, they are found more than 1700 metres down and at night they rise to within 100 metres of the surface. They get their name from the glowing light organs (called photophores) along their body.

Tiger shark

The tiger shark is one of the largest sharks. It hunts mainly at night when it it comes up close to the surface of the water. During the day it goes deeper down into the ocean, usually to around 300 metres.

The tiger shark eats all sorts of marine creatures including dolphins, seals, turtles, fish and even other sharks.

SHARKS IN THE DEEP

Scientists have explored the upper layers of the sea quite thoroughly, but the deep ocean is still a mysterious place. We do not know much about this habitat. Few people have explored it by submarine. However, we do know that sharks live in deep water and can survive down to depths of around 3000 metres.

GOING DOWN

As you descend from the surface, the sea becomes darker and colder. The pressure increases, too. In very deep water, a diver would be crushed and all the air squeezed from their lungs. Only animals adapted to this environment can survive. The surface layer goes down to about 200 metres. Next comes the twilight zone, from 200 to 1000 metres. The midnight zone stretches to the sea bed.

Sunlit zone

Sunlight passes through the water to depths of about 200 metres. Here in the surface layer, there is enough light for plant plankton and seaweeds to make their food.

Nurse sharks spend most of their time in the sunny surface layer of the sea.

Sixgill sharks are found down near the deep sea bed.

Twilight zone

Beneath the surface layer, there is a glimmer of light – just enough for some animals to see. Animals dive down from the surface into this layer for safety.

Midnight zone

The midnight zone is pitch black and cold, and the water is still. Fish and other sea creatures living below 500 metres are designed to withstand the great pressure of the surrounding water.

Sperm whales can stay underwater for well over an hour without taking a breath

Did you know?

Sperm whales can dive to incredible depths. One sperm whale caught by a whaling ship in water 3000 metres deep had a shark in its stomach.

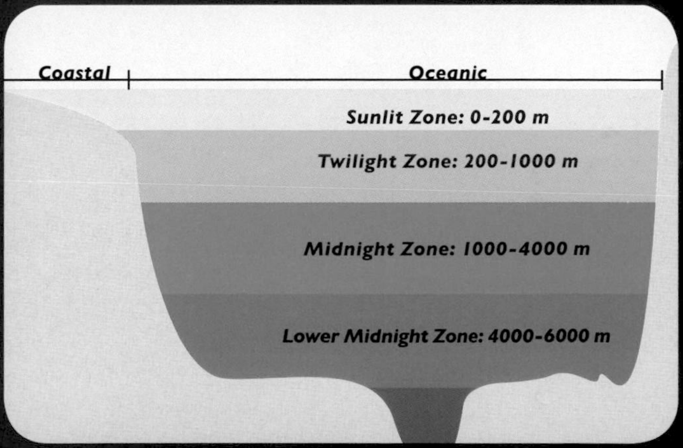

Coastal | *Oceanic*

Sunlit Zone: 0–200 m

Twilight Zone: 200–1000 m

Midnight Zone: 1000–4000 m

Lower Midnight Zone: 4000–6000 m

TWILIGHT ZONE

A variety of animals, from tiny plankton to huge whales, live permanently in the twilight zone. Their bodies are specially adapted for life in deep, gloomy water.

Catsharks

Catsharks are a family of around 150 species. These sharks live in habitats ranging from shallow waters right down to 2000 metres or more. Some of them hunt in the twilight zone for nautilus, cuttlefish and squid.

Did you know?

Frilled sharks live in deep waters in the twilight zone. They are shaped like a snake, with a huge mouth containing around 300 needle-like teeth.

Catshark

Twilight shrimp

The twilight shrimp has a red shell – a colour that is difficult to spot in the gloom. It catches small plankton animals in its claws.

Hatchetfish

A hatchetfish has a flat body. It has light-producing organs on its underside. The lights disguise the fish's shape so it is not spotted by predators in the water below.

Nautilus

The nautilus is a relative of the squid. It has a spiral shell for protection. If necessary, it can disappear inside completely. Its eyes help it to see in the gloom.

The nautilus has many more tentacles than a squid, but no suckers.

Eye

DIVING DEEP

Seals, whales, sharks and penguins are just some of the animals that dive down into the twilight zone and beyond to find food.

Little is known about the megamouth shark, which was first discovered near Hawaii in 1976. Since then, only about 40 megamouths have been seen.

Megamouth

The odd-looking megamouth shark grows to about 7 metres long. It has a metre-wide mouth. Like many ocean animals, it spends the daylight hours in deep water and swims to the surface to feed at night.

Diving birds

Many seabirds, such as penguins, dive underwater to catch food. The penguin is a flightless bird with flippers rather than wings. It is clumsy on land, but an expert swimmer. The emperor penguin spends up to 15 minutes under the water at a time. It dives to depths of about 500 metres.

Weddell seals

The Weddell seal dives at night to find krill, squid and fish. It can stay under the water for up to an hour, reaching depths of about 700 metres before it has to return to the surface to breathe.

Weddell seal

Twilight hunter

The sperm whale dives down to 1000 metres, or more, in search of squid. Scientists believe that the whale produces sound waves to stun its prey.

GOBLIN SHARK

Very little is known about the goblin shark as it lives in the deep ocean. Only about 45 specimens have been studied to date.

Goblin sharks are not often seen because they live in deep water at the bottom of the ocean. They are only seen when they are caught in the fishing nets of deep-sea trawlers. The goblin shark is pink-grey in colour because its blood vessels lie close to the surface of the skin and can be seen through it.

It is very dark in the deep ocean so the goblin shark does not rely on its eyesight to detect prey. Scientists think that special organs on its long snout can detect the faint electrical fields created by other fish and invertebrates when they move. It may also use the snout to dig up fish and crustaceans that are hiding in the sand and silt on the sea floor.

A goblin shark's jaws act like a spring-loaded trap. The teeth and jaws can be catapulted forwards, rather like opening a telescope, to snatch a fish from the water. Then they spring back to their normal position.

Body
The body is soft and quite rubbery. The caudal fin is very long compared to the two dorsal fins.

Profile

Length:	2.4 to 3.2 m (males), 3.1 to 3.5 m (females)
Weight:	Around 180 kg (males and females), 210 kg maximum
Order:	Mackerel sharks
Family:	Goblin sharks
Diet:	Fish, squid (right) and other molluscs, crustaceans

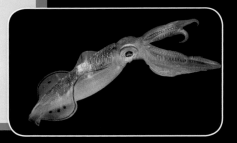

Snout
The large flattened snout protrudes from the top of its head. Beneath this are the jaws with slender fang-like teeth.

Location

Goblin sharks have been found off the coast of Japan, Australia, New Zealand and southern Africa, and in the eastern Atlantic and Indian Oceans. They swim near the sea bottom at about 250 metres deep, but can go down to 1200 metres or more.

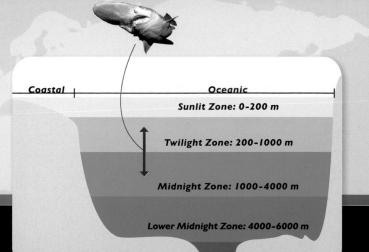

Coastal | Oceanic

Sunlit Zone: 0-200 m

Twilight Zone: 200-1000 m

Midnight Zone: 1000-4000 m

Lower Midnight Zone: 4000-6000 m

THE DEEP

The deep is a cold, eerie place where very little lives. The animals of the deep have all sorts of unusual features, which help them get something to eat in this 'food desert'.

Light in the dark

Sunlight does not penetrate the deep ocean. It is very dark all the time. Many animals in the deep sea have developed organs that can produce light. This is known as bioluminescence. It is used to lure prey, to distract predators and to attract mates.

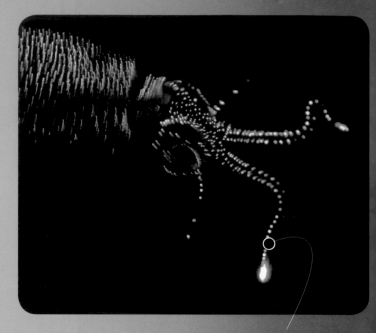

The firefly squid has tiny organs on its tentacles which emit light. This attracts small fish, which the squid eats.

Deep sea medusa

The deep sea medusa is a relative of the jellyfish. It traps prey, such as small shrimps and baby fish, in its long tentacles. It has 22 of them around its body.

Snipe eel

The snipe eel has jaws that do not close. It swims with its mouth open. Small animals, such as amphipods (shrimp-like creatures), are trapped on the teeth and swallowed. The snipe eel grows to over a metre long.

Scuba divers do not normally go deeper than around 40 metres. To explore the deep ocean scientists use manned submersibles or robot vehicles.

Did you know?

The velvet belly lanternshark can give off light. Its photophores (light-producing organs) are arranged in a special pattern. This helps velvet bellies recognise one another in the dark.

Fishing the deep

The angler fish lures its prey with a light that dangles from the end of a spine in front of its large mouth. The light is produced by tiny bacteria.

DEEP SEA SQUID

Many stories have been written about monsters of the deep. In these tales it is said that they have risen from the deep and wrapped their tentacles around boats to pull them down under the water.

One of the most mysterious of the deep sea squids is the giant squid. These animals are rare, and few have been seen alive.

Sometimes, the bodies of giant squid are washed up on beaches. This gives scientists the chance to study them. Their remains have also been found in the stomachs of sperm whales.

Many giant squid can produce their own light. They switch this light on and off to attract fish. When the fish are close enough, the squid grab them.

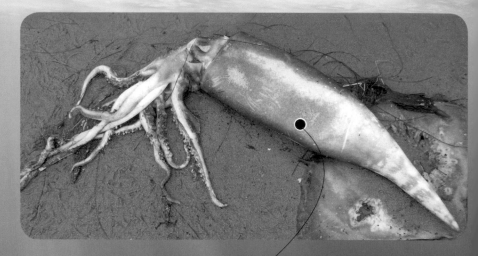

The body of a giant squid washed up on a beach.

Colossal squid

The colossal squid is even larger than the giant squid. It is the world's largest invertebrate animal, reaching a massive 14 metres in length. Its tentacles have razor-like hooks, which can cause injuries to other animals.

This deep sea squid, called *Teuthowenia*, produces its own light to attract prey.

Sleeper sharks

Sleeper sharks live in the cold waters near the North and South poles. Some of the larger species eat giant squid and colossal squid. The sperm whale is the only other animal known to eat these huge squid.

LIFE ON THE SEA BED

Some of the deep sea bed is rocky, but it is mostly covered by a thick layer of mud. This mud contains the remains of dead animals that have dropped from the water above.

Pacific sleeper shark

The Pacific sleeper shark feeds on bottom-dwelling fish, shrimps, crabs and marine snails. Larger sharks can even catch fast-swimming squid, octopuses, salmon and porpoises.

Deep sea spines

The round sea urchin is covered in long spines. Its mouth is on the underside, surrounded by five teeth-like plates. It uses these plates to feed on dead matter and animals such as mussels and sponges.

Sea slug

The sea slug
is a mollusc with
a tube-shaped body,
leathery skin and a ring
of sticky tentacles around its mouth.
It uses its tentacles to find food in the mud.

Sea pens are
related to corals.

Long-legged crabs

Spider crabs scuttle across the deep sea bed in
search of food. They have a small body and 10 very
long legs. They cannot see anything in the dark, so
they use their sense of touch to catch prey.

Did you know?

The sea pen attaches to
the deep sea bed, where it
catches small animals with
its stinging tentacles. Each
sea pen is actually a colony
of individual polyps that
live together.

SIXGILL SHARK

This big shark normally lives in the darkness of the deep oceans at depths down to around 2000 metres.

The sixgill shark ranges in colour from grey, olive green to brown on the upper side, fading to a paler underside. There is a light-coloured stripe along each flank. It has small, teardrop-shaped, green eyes with black pupils.

It normally hunts on its own, swimming slowly and steadily through the water searching for food. When it spots something to eat, it accelerates rapidly to catch its prey. The teeth in its lower jaw are shaped like the blade of a saw. The shark uses them to rip the flesh off the body of large fish that it cannot swallow whole.

Sixgill sharks are not considered dangerous to humans as they are quite shy and not aggressive unless provoked. Also, they generally keep to deep waters where divers cannot follow them.

Gills
Most sharks have five gill slits on each side of their bodies, but the sixgill shark has six long slits.

Profile

Length:	3.1 to 3.3 m long (males), 3.5 to 4.3 m long (females)
Weight:	Average 200 kg (males), 400 kg (females), 590 kg maximum
Order:	Frilled and cow sharks
Family:	Cow sharks
Diet:	Fish, snails, crabs (right), shrimps, squid, some marine mammals

Dorsal fin
There is only one dorsal fin on this shark's back, set quite a long way back towards the tail.

Location

Sixgill sharks are found worldwide in tropical (over 18 °C) and temperate (10 to 18 °C) waters. They usually swim from about 90 metres to as deep as 2000 metres.

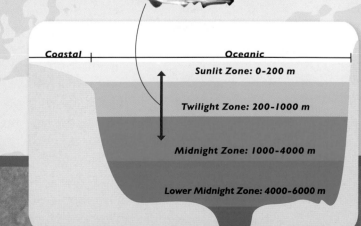

Coastal | Oceanic

Sunlit Zone: 0–200 m

Twilight Zone: 200–1000 m

Midnight Zone: 1000–4000 m

Lower Midnight Zone: 4000–6000 m

DEEP SEA WORMS

Worms are invertebrate animals with a long, soft, boneless body. There are all sorts of marine worms including tapeworms and fan worms. Sharks and rays that live near the sea bed feed on worms.

Undersea parasites

Parasites are animals that live in, and do harm to, other animals. The tapeworm is a common parasite in many deep sea fish. The tapeworm lives and feeds in the fish's gut. Tapeworms spread when their eggs are eaten by small creatures, like crustaceans. These are part of the food chain, and are eaten in turn by larger fish. Eventually a shark will eat the fish that contains the tapeworm parasites and become infected itself.

Blue sharks commonly have parasites inside them.

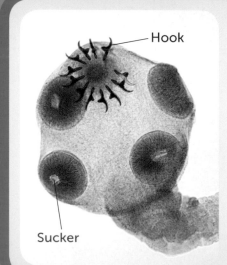

Hook

Sucker

Tapeworms

Tapeworms are parasites that live inside the guts of all types of shark. Tapeworms use their hooks and suckers to grip the inside of the gut, where they absorb food. When the guts of 24 dead blue sharks were cut open, scientists found that each shark contained hundreds of tapeworms inside its guts.

Tube worm

The tentacles of this deep sea worm look a bit like spaghetti. The worm extends these sticky tentacles over the sea bed to catch any small particles that sink down from above. If danger threatens, the worm pulls the tentacles back into its body.

Catching food

Fan worms are found on the deep sea bed. Their soft body is protected by a hard, bony tube. They extend a ring of sticky tentacles from the top of the tube to catch small animals drifting in the water. If disturbed, fan worms can shoot back inside their tubes.

Did you know?

Sometimes parasites can do good. Worms in the gut of whitecheek sharks absorb high doses of toxic metals like cadmium and lead. So the worms are filtering out these poisons before they harm the sharks.

FOOD AND SHELTER

When the body of a large animal drops to the sea bed, scavengers come from far and wide to feed upon it. Other animals take shelter among objects that find their way to the sea bed.

There is a constant supply of 'marine snow' from the waters above. This 'snow' is the broken-down remains of dead plants and animals – especially plankton. These tiny remains drift slowly to the sea bed where they become an important source of food for bottom-dwellers.

Spiny dogfish shark

Finding shelter

Animals on the sea bed need shelter from predators. Many hide among bones, or even old cans and objects that have dropped to the sea bed. Unfortunately, deep-sea trawling nets can sweep away these tiny shelters.

Did you know?

Sharks usually eat live prey rather than scavenging on the sea floor. But the spiny dogfish shark is a bottom-dwelling scavenger. It has two sharp poisonous spines on its back to keep other predators away.

Hagfish

The hagfish looks a bit like an eel. It is a scavenger that lives on the ocean floor. The hagfish burrows into the bodies of dead animals and eats them from the inside out. It is an unusual fish because it does not have jaws or teeth. Instead, it has a very rough tongue.

Brittle star

The brittle star has five long arms, which it uses to pull itself across the sea bed. It sometimes preys on small shrimps and other animals, but mostly scavenges on dead matter.

STARFISH

Starfish are spiny-skinned animals that belong to a group of animals called echinoderms. They are related to sea urchins, sea cucumbers, seastars and brittle stars.

Most starfish have five or more arms, called rays, joined to a central body. The mouth is on the underside. Starfish eat by pouring the acid from their stomach on to their food. The acid dissolves the food so the starfish can digest it.

To move, a starfish swings each ray forward then pushes down, pulling itself along. There is a tiny sucker at the end of each ray, to grip. The starfish also uses the sucker to force open the shells of mussels and clams.

If a starfish loses one of its rays, it can grow a new one. This process is called regeneration.

Sensing light and dark

Starfish do not have eyes like fish do, but they have eyespots at the end of each ray. These are primitive sensors that can detect light and dark.

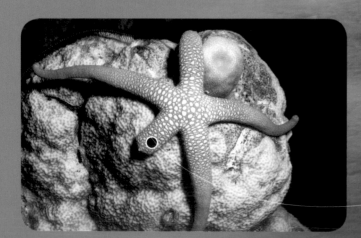

Starfish can regrow their rays.

Horn sharks

Bottom-dwelling species such as horn sharks eat starfish. The horn shark uses its front teeth to grab the starfish, then crushes it with its back teeth before swallowing it.

Starfish move slowly, which makes them easy prey for sharks, squid and octopuses.

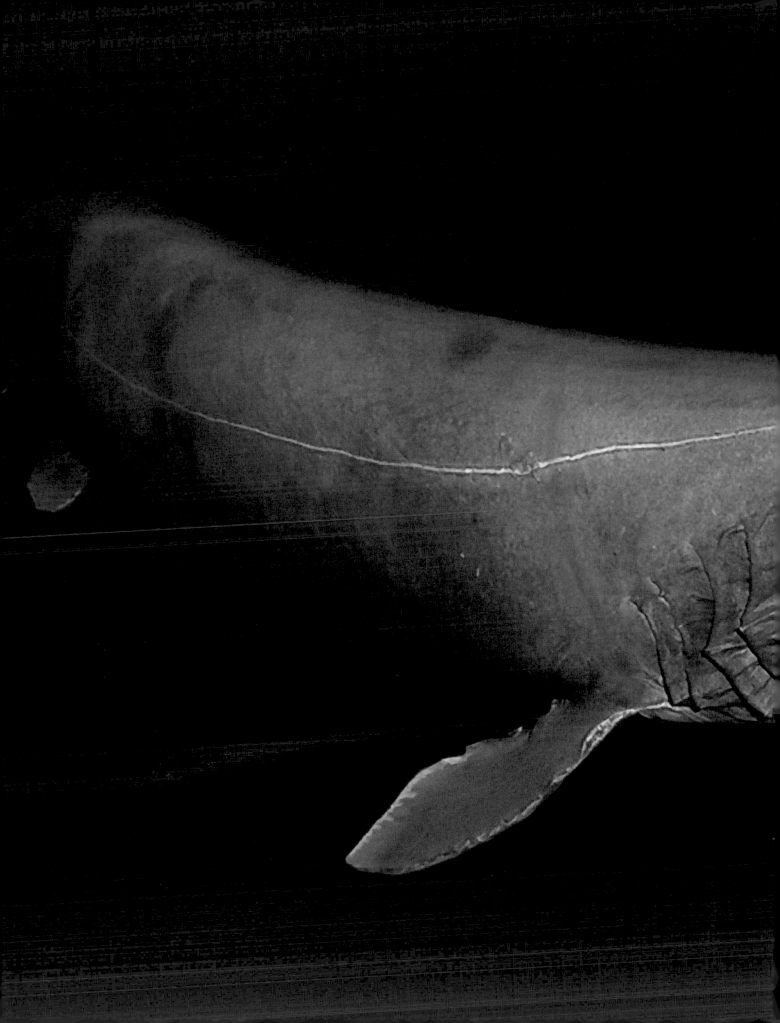

Frilled shark

The frilled shark is a strange serpent-like shark that grows to over 1 metre long. It lives in the deep sea, often at depths below 1000 metres. It has around 300 spear-like teeth which it uses to grasp slippery squid. It gets its name from the frilly edges of its six rows of gills.

SEA BED FISH

A surprising number of fish are found on the deep sea bed, and more are being discovered all the time. They have been given unusual names such as the rat-tail, cookie-cutter shark and even the blobfish.

The cookie-cutter shark has a bioluminescent patch on its belly. Hunting fish think it is harmless as they can only see the small patch in the dark. When they come close, the cookie-cutter ambushes them.

Cookie-cutter shark

This shark was first discovered off the coast of Brazil in the 1820s. It lives in deep water below 1000 metres. It gets its name from the round scars that it leaves on its prey. It grips its prey in its mouth and, using its long teeth, pulls out a lump of flesh leaving behind a nasty hole.

Deep sea blob

The blobfish was discovered in 2003, on a sea bed 1200 metres deep. Little is known about it, but the shape of its mouth suggests that it eats whatever it can find.

The blobfish lives in deep waters off the coast of Australia.

Sixgill shark

The sixgill shark is found at depths of up to 2000 metres, where it rests during the day. At night, it swims to the surface to hunt for fish and seals.

Sixgill shark

Deep sea rat-tail

The rat-tail, or grenadier, is one of the most common deep sea fish. It has a large head, a slender body and, unusually, no tail fin. These fish live in water up to 5000 metres deep, where they hunt animals such as smaller fish and shrimps.

DEEP OCEAN CLIFFS

There are cliffs, mountains and trenches in the deep ocean.
These are home to many animals, including corals and sponges.

Deep sea coral

Not all corals are found in
shallow, warm, tropical seas.
Many corals live in cold,
deep water. Some live as
deep as 1000 metres. Deep
sea reefs grow very slowly,
and some are hundreds of
years old.

Deep sea coral

Deep sea sponges

Some deep-water
sponges have a skeleton
that is made from glass.
They produce tiny
pieces of glass, which
stick together to form a
beautiful skeleton that
is strong enough to
support their body.

Hiding in cracks

The wolf fish, or seawolf, pushes its body
backwards into the cracks of a cliff. It leaves
its head sticking out, watching for prey. It has a
wide mouth with large pointed teeth, which it
uses to feed on clams, mussels and starfish.

A wolf fish hiding in
a hole in the rocks.

Cliff hugger

Sea anemones, and other animals that cannot swim, cling tightly to the cliff. If they let go, they could sink into the deep below.

Divers can explore cliffs that lie close to the surface. Mini-submarines are needed for the deep ocean.

Did you know?

The Portuguese shark holds the world record for the deepest caught shark. Most live at around 1000 metres but several have been caught right down at around 3000 metres.

SHARKS AND PEOPLE

Although sharks have been living in the Earth's oceans for more than 400 million years, in recent years their future has become threatened. This is because human beings have started to affect what happens to creatures in the ocean, leading to a serious decline in the number of sharks.

SHARK FISHING

Many sharks are known as apex predators. This means that they kill and eat other animals but that virtually no predators in the oceans kill them. However, sharks do have one deadly enemy that lives on land – humans.

Commercial fishing

Every year, around 100 million sharks are caught and killed. This is because a lot of people earn their living by catching sharks. Shark products, including meat, the fins, the skin and the teeth, are sold in huge quantities.

Unwanted victims

Sharks are often caught in trawler nets or on longline hooks that have been set to catch other fish, such as tuna or swordfish. The sharks die even though the fisherman do not want them. They are known as 'bycatch'.

Sport fishing

In certain parts of the world the sport of fishing for big game fish is very popular. Some fishermen release the fish after it has been caught and photographed, but others kill their catch to keep as a trophy.

Sharks are one of the game fish that sports fishermen try to catch using fast boats like this.

Shark's fin soup

A thick soup made from shark fins is very popular in the Far East. It is thought to have medicinal properties. Some fishermen catch sharks, cut off their fins and then throw the sharks back in the water. Millions die in this way.

GETTING CLOSE TO SHARKS

Many people are curious about sharks — they are big, powerful and fascinating animals. There are different ways that we can see them up-close.

Diving with sharks

In the clear, warm waters of the tropics, diving with sharks has become a tourist attraction. Some dive companies even organize shark feeds to attract sharks to a particular spot.

In the aquarium

One way that people can get close to sharks is to visit one of the many aquariums that display them to the public. As well as providing a tourist attraction, these sealife centres allow scientists to study shark behaviour in order to help protect them.

Did you know?

The Ocean Voyager tank at Georgia Aquarium in the United States is the largest aquarium habitat in the world. It contains more than 6 million gallons of salt water. It is large enough to be a home for whale sharks.

Shark cages

The great white shark is seen as the ultimate man-eater. It is now possible for tourists to watch great whites from inside the safety of a submerged metal cage.

Great white shark

On the screen

Television has had a huge impact on our knowledge of sharks. Nature programmes give us an insight into their behaviour and habits. Films like *Jaws* and *Deep Blue Sea* portray the shark as a deadly monster.

Divers can take photographs of huge sharks while safe inside the cage.

GREAT WHITE SHARK

The huge and aggressive great white is the most dangerous shark in the world. It has attacked more swimmers, surfers, divers and small boats than any other species of shark.

A great white shark's body is streamlined and shaped like a torpedo. Despite its name, only its belly is actually white; the top is grey or blue-grey. This is useful when hunting its prey because the great white usually strikes from below – to its prey above, its grey colour blends in with the dark water.

The shark's target is normally attacked in a surprise rush and bitten once to stun it. Sometimes, the shark will leap out of the water because of the speed and power of its attack. When the victim is stunned and dying, the shark returns to feed.

The great white is the only shark that pokes its head out of the water. It may be to spot prey swimming on the surface, such as seals and sea lions.

Pectoral fins
Large sickle-shaped pectoral fins help the shark to steer through the water.

Profile

Length:	3.5 to 4 m (males), 4.5 to 5 m (females), 6.8 m maximum
Weight:	Average 700 to 1800 kg (males and females), 3200 kg maximum
Order:	Mackerel sharks
Family:	Mackerel sharks
Diet:	Fish including other sharks, seals, sea lions, dolphins, small whales, sea turtles

Nostrils
An incredible sense of smell can detect one drop of blood in 100 litres of water, and sense blood up to 5 kilometres away.

Teeth
Around 300 huge, triangular, jagged teeth – each one as long as a human finger.

Location
Great white sharks are found worldwide in temperate (10 to 18 °C) waters, and some also are found in tropical (over 18 °C) waters. They swim from the surface to 2000 metres.

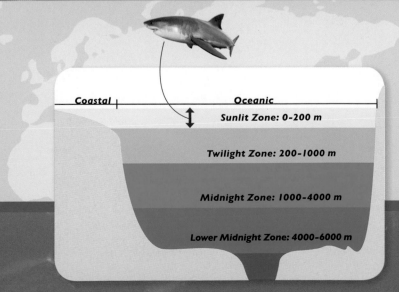

Coastal | Oceanic

Sunlit Zone: 0–200 m

Twilight Zone: 200–1000 m

Midnight Zone: 1000–4000 m

Lower Midnight Zone: 4000–6000 m

SHARK ATTACKS

Whenever a shark attacks someone swimming offshore, it makes news all around the world, particularly if the victim is killed. But most experts agree that the risk of being attacked by a shark is very small.

Attacks are rare

Worldwide there are only around 70 to 100 attacks in an average year, of which around 10 to 15 are fatal. More people are killed by bees each year than by sharks.

Surfing star

In October 2003, 13-year-old Bethany Hamilton was surfing off the coast of Hawaii when she was attacked by a tiger shark. It bit off her left arm. She survived the attack and returned to the water 26 days later. In 2007, she became a professional surfer.

When sharks attack surfers, they probably mistake the outline of the surfboard for prey.

Survivor

One of world's leading authorities on the great white shark, Rodney Fox, was himself the victim of a terrible attack in 1963. He was almost bitten in half and his wounds needed more than 450 stitches. Since then he has dedicated his life to the appreciation and preservation of the great white shark.

A fighting chance

Anyone who is unlucky enough to be attacked by a shark should try to fight back by hitting the shark on its snout and clawing at its eyes and gills.

The eyes and snout are a shark's vulnerable areas.

Great white shark

A great white breaks the surface of the water as it hunts for food. These are the largest predatory fish in the oceans. Their bite is about twice as powerful as that of a lion.

OCEANS IN DANGER

The oceans are important to people. We transport essential goods on them by ship and get food and natural resources from the sea. However, we also damage the oceans through pollution and over-fishing, and this creates problems for sharks.

Sharks sometimes become tangled in nets and die.

Dangers of pollution

When there is an oil spill or when waste materials are dumped at sea, humans are contributing to the pollution of the oceans. Pollution can contaminate fish that come into contact with it. When sharks eat contaminated fish, they end up with high levels of dangerous chemicals in their bodies.

Accidents at sea often lead to ocean pollution.

Polluting sewage

Millions of litres of sewage are emptied into the oceans each year by people. Fish that live in coastal waters can be harmed by sewage. This also harms sharks that feed on the fish living in these waters.

Did you know?

Some tourist resorts put shark nets off the shoreline to keep sharks away from the beach. Sharks, turtles, dolphins and rays can all get tangled and die in these nets.

Rubbish dumped at sea

Waste material thrown into the sea includes discarded fishing lines, nets and plastics in which sharks sometimes get entangled. If they cannot get free, they will die in the water.

Not many young

Sharks are slow to mature and may produce just a few young in any breeding cycle. This means that when populations are hit by over-fishing or ocean pollution, the numbers take a very long time to recover.

SHORTFIN MAKO SHARK

This is one of the fastest sharks in the ocean. It can reach speeds of up to 50 kilometres per hour when chasing after prey and can leap clear out of the water to heights of up to 6 metres.

The shortfin mako shark's upper side is metallic blue while the underside is white. This pattern is known as countershading. It makes the shark hard to spot in the water when seen both from above and from below.

The shortfin mako's speed allows it to feed on quick-moving fish, such as tuna, swordfish and even other sharks. It is able to hunt them because it swims faster than they do.

Due to their size and speed, shortfin makos can be dangerous to humans. There have been a number of attacks on swimmers and divers and some of them have been fatal. Divers have reported that the shark will swim in a figure-of-eight pattern before launching an attack with its mouth open.

Body shape
Sleek and streamlined with a long, cone-shaped snout. It slips easily through the water, which helps the shark to swim so fast.

Profile

Length:	Average 1.8 to 2.5 m (males and females), 3.9 m maximum
Weight:	Average 60 to 135 kg (males and females), 570 kg maximum
Order:	Mackerel sharks
Family:	Mackerel sharks
Diet:	Fish including other sharks, rays, squid, dolphins (right), small whales

Teeth

Slender, slightly curved and pointed teeth, with razor-sharp edges, help the mako grip slippery, fast-moving fish.

Location

Shortfin mako sharks are found worldwide in warm temperate (16 to 18 °C) and tropical (over 18 °C) waters. They swim from the surface to 150 metres.

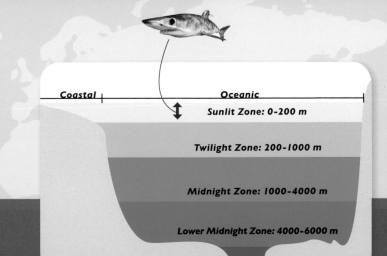

Coastal | Oceanic

Sunlit Zone: 0–200 m

Twilight Zone: 200–1000 m

Midnight Zone: 1000–4000 m

Lower Midnight Zone: 4000–6000 m

GLOBAL WARMING

Global warming is the gradual increase in temperature of the Earth's atmosphere. Scientists believe that this will cause climates to change, sea levels to rise and extreme weather to become more common.

Changing habits

As the sea gets warmer, some marine animals change their behaviour. They appear in places where they have not been seen before. Scientists believe that some time this century sharks will begin to be seen in the ocean around Antarctica.

Did you know?

The oceans are important to our planet because they absorb carbon dioxide from the atmosphere. Sharks are a vital part of the marine habitat because they keep life in the oceans in healthy balance.

Reefs in danger

Warming seas around coral reefs can cause devastation. The coral dies and turns white. This deprives reef fish of food and shelter and their population drops. This, in turn, means the reef sharks struggle to find food.

Polluting the atmosphere

Global warming is thought to be caused by an increase in greenhouse gases such as carbon dioxide. These gases trap heat in the atmosphere. Carbon dioxide is produced when oil, gas and coal are burnt.

What can we do?

Everybody can help to slow down global warming by walking and cycling as this does not burn oil. If we travel in aeroplanes, buses or cars, carbon dioxide is produced, which may speed up global warming.

Beautiful natural habitats like this coral reef are threatened by rising sea temperatures.

PROTECTING SHARKS

Although changes in the world's weather, the effects of pollution and the impact of fishing all spell danger for sharks, many people are trying to protect and conserve shark populations around the globe.

Shark sanctuaries

Some countries have banned commercial fishing in their national waters (the parts of the sea that they control) to help protect sharks. The island groups of Palau, in the western Pacific Ocean, and the Maldives, in the Indian Ocean, have both done this.

Palau, a country made up of around 250 Pacific islands, has created a protected area for sharks.

Acting responsibly

Tourists who want to see and swim with sharks should make sure that the dive company treats sharks with proper care.

How can we help?

We can help sharks to survive in the wild by not buying shark products, which encourages shark fishing. We can also try to persuade the politicians to change the laws that govern how commercial fishing is done. Some people are trying to get laws changed so that sharks are better protected.

Better understanding

Scientific research, sealife visitor centres, television programmes, magazine articles, films and books all help the general public to understand that sharks are remarkable creatures.

Scientists tag a shortfin mako shark to help track its migrations.

Did you know?

Scientists in New Zealand have tagged a mako shark so that it can be tracked by satellite. It travelled more than 13,300 kilometres in 7 months, sometimes swimming more than 100 kilometres in a day.

Aquariums are great places to learn about sharks and see them close up.

Whale shark
A whale shark glides through the water surrounded by several smaller fish and almost as many scuba divers.

USEFUL WORDS

Algae
Organisms that are mostly found in water and are generally very small.

Amphipod
A tiny shrimp-like crustacean that lives in the water.

Aquatic
Relating to water. Aquatic animals all live in water.

Baleen
Sieve-like material in the mouths of some whales. Used to filter feed.

Barbel
Whisker-like feelers near the nostrils and mouth of some sharks. Used to taste and feel.

Bioluminescence
The ability of a living organism to produce light.

Bivalve
A mollusc that has two shells, which are hinged together.

Camouflage
A special colouring or body shape that blends with the surroundings so that an animal is not easily seen by predators or prey.

Carnivore
An animal that eats other animals.

Cartilage
Tough, light and stretchy material from which a shark's skeleton is made.

Colony
A group of animals living together.

Continental shelf
The sea floor that slopes gradually from a continent down to a depth of about 200 metres.

Copepod
A tiny shrimp-like crustacean that lives in the water.

Crustacean
An invertebrate animal that has an outer shell (an exoskeleton) and jointed legs. Such as lobsters, crabs and shrimps.

Diatom
A type of plant plankton with a hard shell-like skeleton made of two halves.

Dorsal fin
The tall fin that stands upright on a shark's back.

Echinoderms
Marine animals that have arms or rays, such as starfish and sea urchins.

Equator
An imaginary line that runs around the Earth's surface, halfway between the two poles.

Frond
The leaf-like part of a seaweed.

Gill
The parts of the body used by fish and some other animals to allow them to breathe underwater.

Gravity
The force that attracts objects towards large bodies, like the Earth or Sun.

Habitat
The name given to the place where an animal or plant lives.

Invertebrate
An animal that does not have a backbone.

Kelp
Large seaweeds that grow in underwater forests in shallow seas.

Lagoon
An area of salty water cut off from the sea by a bank of shingle, sand or coral.

Larva
The growing stage of an animal such as a young fish or squid.

Mammal
A warm-blooded animal. Female mammals give birth to live young and feed them with their own milk.

Marine
To do with the sea.

Microscopic
Too small to be seen with the naked eye.

Migration
A regular journey made by an animal, sometimes over very long distances.

Mollusc
An animal with a soft body, usually protected by an outer shell.

Mucus
A thick slimy fluid that an organism produces to protect itself.

Nocturnal
Being active at night rather than during the day.

Nutrient
A substance that is needed for healthy growth and living.

Organism
A living thing such as an animal, plant, fungus or bacterium.

Parasite
An animal that lives off another animal (the host) without doing anything to benefit the host.

Pectoral fins
The fins that stick out of the sides of a shark's body just behind its gills.

Photosynthesis
The process by which plants use sunlight and the green chlorophyll in their leaves to make sugars that give the plant energy.

Phytoplankton
Tiny plants that float freely in the ocean currents.

Plankton
The tiny plants and animals that are found floating close to the surface of ponds, lakes and seas.

Polar
To do with the areas around the North and South Poles.

Pollution
The act of making something, like the air or the water, unclean by discharging harmful substances into it.

Population
The number of individuals living in a particular area.

Predator
An animal that hunts and feeds on other animals.

Prey
An animal that is hunted by other animals.

Pupil
The central part of an eye that lets in light.

Respiratory system
The parts of a body that allow an organism to breathe.

Sensor
Part of an organism that responds to a particular stimulus, such as light, sound or heat.

Shoal
A group of fish that swim together.

Solitary
A plant or animal that lives alone.

Sonar
A way of finding the position of objects or prey by using sound waves that travel through the water.

Streamlined
Having a shape that slips easily through air or a liquid, like a torpedo for instance.

Structure
The way something is built or put together.

Submersible
A vessel used for undersea exploration. It can have a human crew, or be unmanned.

Swimbladder
A gas-filled organ inside a fish that stops it from sinking in the water.

Tentacle
A long, feeler-like structure found on certain animals, such as jellyfish, anemones and squid.

Tropical
Relating to a part of the Earth that lies close to the Equator. The climate in the tropical zone is hot and wet for most of the year.

Tsunami
A big wave created by an earthquake happening under the ocean.

Vertebrate
An animal that has a backbone.

Zooplankton
Tiny animals that float freely in the ocean currents.

INDEX

Picture credits